A Walk in
Our Shoes

A Walk in
Our Shoes

Helena C. Farrell
and
Geralyn A. Mancini

authorHOUSE®

AuthorHouse™ LLC
1663 Liberty Drive
Bloomington, IN 47403
www.authorhouse.com
Phone: 1-800-839-8640

© 2013 by Helena C. Farrell and Geralyn A. Mancini. All rights reserved.

No part of this book may be reproduced, stored in a retrieval system, or transmitted by any means without the written permission of the author.

Published by AuthorHouse   10/25/2013

ISBN: 978-1-4918-1943-2 (sc)
ISBN: 978-1-4772-6642-7 (hc)
ISBN: 978-1-4918-1942-5 (e)

Library of Congress Control Number: 2013916930

Any people depicted in stock imagery provided by Thinkstock are models, and such images are being used for illustrative purposes only.
Certain stock imagery © Thinkstock.

This book is printed on acid-free paper.

Because of the dynamic nature of the Internet, any web addresses or links contained in this book may have changed since publication and may no longer be valid. The views expressed in this work are solely those of the author and do not necessarily reflect the views of the publisher, and the publisher hereby disclaims any responsibility for them.

Deena and Jeffrey Leider's Journey

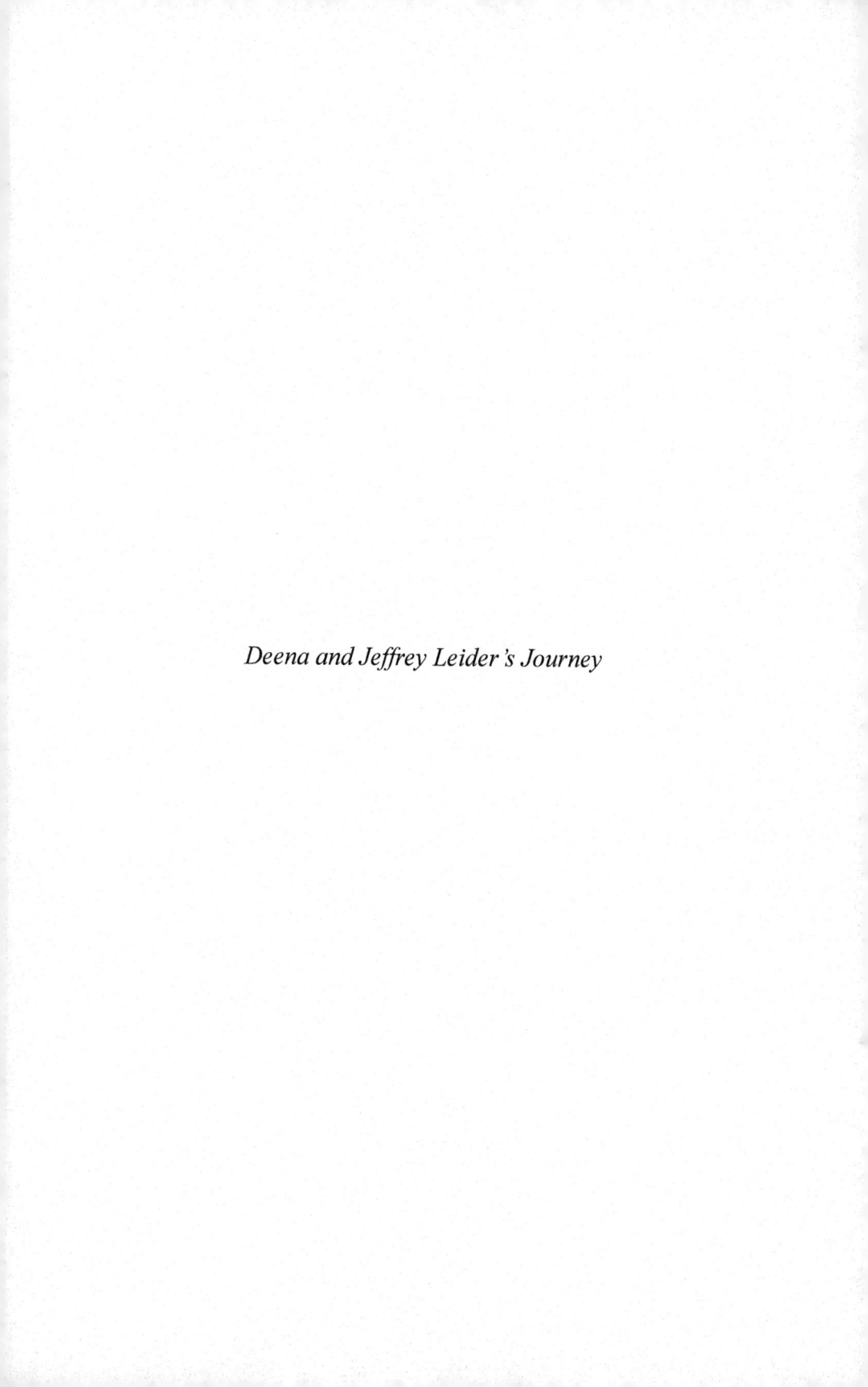

For
Jason and Justin our treasured sons
and
our precious daughter, Jordan

It is good to have an end to journey toward,

but it is the journey that matters,

in the end.

~Ernest Hemingway

CHAPTER ONE

The probability that we may fail in the struggle
Ought not to deter us from
The support of a cause we believe to be just;
It shall not deter me.

~ Abraham Lincoln

IT'S A BRIGHT blustery February morning in our nation's capital in 2012. As the sun begins to rise, it casts a soft golden light on the imposing historical monuments. These monuments illuminate and glorify America's proud history and honor our past presidents and gallant war heroes; lest we forget their major struggles and contributions. The memory of Abraham Lincoln is enshrined forever by the Lincoln Memorial. It majestically and protectively looms over the beautiful Reflecting Pool reminding us of how humble men and women have bravely changed the course of the world and transformed and saved so many lives. I haven't visited here since 1977, yet I am still impressed and awed by its affect on me.

While walking with a friend by one of the monuments, a family with a healthy vibrant young boy asks if one of us would take a photo of them. As my friend obliges, I watch them pose and the painful reminder of my own family's struggles invade my thoughts. When I look at the healthy-looking little boy, I can't help but think about my sons and their condition. It makes me sad but I quickly change my view, reminding myself that there is no time for self-pity. Once again, I am enthralled and motivated by these impressive marble figures and monuments. I've come to the realization that men and women of valor will be my guide and motivators on this journey.

CHAPTER TWO

Purpose is the destination of a vision.
It energizes that vision, gives it force and drive.
It should be positive and powerful and
Serve the better angels of an organization.

~Colin Powell

PRESIDENT OBAMA'S RE-ELECTION campaign and the Republican Party's Presidential nominations are heating up and currently consuming our country's political stage as the Presidential Election for 2012 is creeping upon us. Not that I am uninterested, but this is not my purpose for coming here. I've come as a concerned person for the future of my fellow man and as a father who has a vision for change. Hopefully, the political and personal will merge here for me in my quest for resolution, healing, awareness, and hope.

The Halls of Congress is my destination. I am here as a proud father, an every-day guy—*an average Joe*. My objective is personal and global. I'm filled with an all-consuming mission. As I walk the long corridor, I'm aware of the impact of my clacking shoes on the tiled floors, yet the fierce pounding of my heart is drowning out the noise. The infinite time clock ticking in my pre-occupied brain signals life's fragility for my family and me. All I keep murmuring is, *"Let them be Little."* This mantra is what I fiercely hold on to; it is like a guiding roadmap on this voyage. It assists me in navigating the rugged path that we have traveled this past and unfathomable year.

When I look around, I observe a diverse group of people walking, mingling, and sharing their stories in these hallowed and venerated halls. Some are smiling, others are crying, a few are filled with rage and anger, and sadly, several are resigned. I am keenly and passionately aware of their emotions and goals but I am determined not to let their overpowering energy or disillusionment deter me from *my* mission.

My journey has been arduous and excruciating, yet ironically empowering. The passion that ignites me for this very personal and worthy cause also serves to quell the overwhelming emotional stress. My thoughts about my little boys' dire situation turn to the family we met in front of the monument the day before. Remembering their lively healthy little boy fills me with overwhelming sorrow for my sons who have not been granted that gift. It is difficult to control these emotions, so to avoid becoming more melancholy, I quickly tap into the healing energy that drives me. Concentrating on why I came here and what I hope to accomplish is a definite mood changer.

I take a long, deep breath, as I approach a huge oak-paneled door to the chamber where politically powerful men and women will determine my fate and advocacy. My voice must be heard in such a way that my urgent agenda will become a permanent law. *"Let Them Be Little"* must resonate not only in these chambers, or with my current audience, but also echo resoundingly *around the world!*

Behind the imposing door is Congressman Steve Rothman, D-NJ. After exchanging professional and personal pleasantries, I share with him the purpose and goals for this meeting. I speak from the heart with passion, urgency, and determination while fighting to maintain my composure. Congressman Rothman listens attentively and appears to be clearly moved as we both shed tears by story end. After our meeting, he hugs and reassures me that he will be there for my family and me. I leave the Congressman with a feeling of anticipated hope. Congressman Rothman proved to be an incredible source of inspiration and encouragement. The political and personal merge with mutual respect and understanding of the importance of my mission. There is not going to be a silver lining at the end of this story but anything worth changing is never easy.

CHAPTER THREE

I was born in a small town
And I live in a small town
And that's good enough for me.
                    ~John Cougar Mellencamp

I NEVER IMAGINED my life would end up this way. I was just your typical guy growing up in the small town of Elmwood Park, NJ. I was the youngest of three sons and was blessed with the support of two loving parents. My days were spent shooting hoops, hunting, fishing, riding quads, and counting the days until my *adored Dallas Cowboys* would take the field. Upon finishing high school, my love for the outdoors prompted me to start my own landscaping business. I was also a DJ and performed frequently at many local venues while *hitting* the club scene wearing my Armani clothes and showing off my *sexy* landscaping tan. *Loving life and having a blast!*

Eventually I began to feel "the scene" was getting old as my desire to settle down was getting greater. Always having a love for children, I was anxious to become the *ultimate family guy*. I was starting to feel I would never meet *the right one*. I decided to reach out to my school-teacher cousin, Karen. I asked her to introduce me to one of her available *attractive/smart* teacher friends. Karen did not miss the beat and recommended her colleague and friend, Deena. She said she would be "perfect for me."

Deena Pizzichetta was also from Bergen County. Coincidentally, she grew up in Garfield the town next to mine. She also shared a love for children and had a strong sense of family (Deena could not wait to be a mother). She realized at a young age that she wanted to be a teacher and work with children. I knew we would fit well together but she needed some convincing. This *reluctant* teacher, I was told, was "done with the dating scene" and for her, "a blind date sounded horrible." After much convincing from Karen and Deena's best-friend Iris, we made a date. Deena suggested our first date be on a work night. I found out later this was her strategy for ending the date early if there were "compatibility issues." *Fortunately for me, we hit it off perfectly!*

CHAPTER FOUR

*It had to be you; It had to be you,
I've wandered around, finally found somebody who
Could make me be true . . .
Cause nobody else gave me a thrill . . .*
~Frank Sinatra

WE AGREED TO meet at my place, which I considered a *chick magnet.* I placed lighted fragrant candles everywhere, casting a *dreamy* hue all over my bachelor pad. *Surely, my attention to decorating detail would put most men to shame.* Deena arrived and immediately scoped my apartment, which I naively thought impressed her. *Being the charmer that I am,* I daringly gave her a full tour convinced she would see me as *a true romantic.* Afterward, I found out that she thought my apartment looked like "the home of Martha Stewart." She was pretty emphatic that all those fancy accent pillows were over the top and not usually found in a typical male's apartment. *Really? One of them was a Dallas Cowboys' pillow! Guess men never know what women are thinking.*

So much for trying to seduce her! *Wow, was my typical unshakable male, macho ego shot down—but only temporarily.* Eventually, my charm overwhelmed her and I, in turn, was captivated by her inner and outer beauty. My charisma and *great looks* captured her heart, but our shared, strong sense of family, and our desire to have children, brought us together and sealed our mutual love. Two years later, in September 2004, we got engaged. *Our lives were looking good!*

CHAPTER FIVE

How Sweet it is to be Loved by You.
I needed the shelter of someone's arms,
and there you were.
I needed someone to understand my ups and downs,
and there you were.

~James Taylor

DEENA AND I were married August, 5, 2005 in St. Clements Episcopal Church in Hawthorne, NJ. Our wedding party was dramatic—*classy* black tuxedos for me and the groomsmen and sophisticated satin-black dresses for the bridesmaids. *We were a spectacular and stunning looking bridal party!* The entire group was made up of our wonderful family and friends who have loved and supported us throughout our courtship. We were honored and thrilled that they were part of our very special day; and they have continued to be a vital part of our current lives in good and bad times. Among all that *chic* black, I was immediately awestruck when in contrast, in the back of the church, I spotted this illuminating, breathtaking vision of white. Seeing Deena walk down the aisle took my breath away. She looked beautiful. *What a lucky guy!*

Deena's maid-of-honor was her best friend, Iris, the one who convinced her to go out with me. *Thanks, Iris.* I had a difficult time choosing one best man, therefore (typical for *unconventional me)*, I had three. After saying our vows, the minister's pronouncement of "husband and wife" drew tears from many in the church, *including me. I certainly didn't need to be told twice to kiss my lovely bride!* We kissed to a rousing applause. Arm-in-arm and beaming broadly, Mr. and Mrs. Jeffrey Leider proudly walked down (*I strutted*) that *hell-of-a-long aisle,* as our family and friends clapped and cheered. Dignified and magnificent Deena charmed everyone as she greeted our guests at the back of the church. I was elated and more than eager to begin the celebration and *party like a rock star. Party I did!*

As the guests arrived to the reception, everyone was in a festive, celebratory mood. Deena immediately rushed to check out all the details. The *infamous wedding cake* immediately became her obsessive focus. We ordered a cake with a landscape theme since I was in that business. To be honest, I was thrilled with the idea but Deena—not so much. The end result was labeled a "horrific cake," by my flustered bride. The monstrosity had a waterfall in it and looked like it was from the 1970s—*again Deena's take on it.* She claimed it was *our* version of the "Big Fat Greek Wedding" since it had Greek Columns holding up the different layers with lights and *that ridiculous* waterfall. All Deena wanted was a three-level square cake with ribbons and pearls to match the invitations, "a simple-elegant confection." When she first spotted *it,* she said she thought *it* was a joke. *Now I like to joke about it, but I knew better on our wedding day.*

The wedding cake upset Deena so much that she initially refused to go through the tradition cutting-of-the-wedding cake ceremony (*all she wanted to do was smash the hideous thing*). However, her resolve broke. Her wish was to give each of our future children a photo of our cake cutting just like the ones our parents had given to us from their respective weddings. Deena didn't want to draw any more attention to that "gaudy" mishap; therefore, the cake cutting was quick and uneventful—a simple photo op. To make matters worse, by the time we posed for the shot, I had a few too many and didn't remember doing it. Later when we received our wedding proofs, I was shocked to see that we actually did go through with the tradition and foolishly asked, "We cut the cake?" Needless to say, the question drew a not so nice response.

Our goal for our wedding reception was for our guests to fully enjoy themselves, which meant eating, drinking, and dancing the night away. By the end of the evening, very few guests were sober. The tequila was flowing all night. A continuous slide show of our lives—past and present played throughout the affair. There were over 1400 action shots and the videographer claims that it was the most he has ever seen at a wedding reception. We hired a DJ from Brooklyn to perform at our rollicking affair. Before we booked them, Deena and I instructed the DJ to visit and observe the summer, happy hour at D'Jais, a popular and hopping Belmar, NJ shore bar. This is the action, music, and entertainment we wanted for our wedding reception. The DJ came through with cranked up dancing music—no slow songs or doo wop played the whole night. We wanted the dance floor filled to capacity. Dancing feet, with shoes on or off, was what we wanted. Deena even joined me and played percussion to a Def Leppard song (maybe it was *"Wasted"*). *Belmar's D'Jais definitely had nothing on our rock'n wedding reception.*

Besides, after seeing Deena walk down the aisle, the second most memorable sight for me was the Dallas Cowboy Ice Sculpture situated front and center at the cocktail hour. My beautiful, thoughtful bride surprised me with it. When I first laid eyes on the huge sculpture, *I flipped out*. Proof of this can be seen in our wedding photos where I'm kissing it (*perhaps even more passionately than our first kiss in front of the minister*). Deena and I danced the first dance as husband and wife to James Taylor's "How Sweet it Is." I insisted that we take dance lessons before the big day so I asked my cousin, Donna, a professional dancer, to choreograph the number. Everyone hooted and hollered as I lifted and dipped my dancing bride. "He always needs to be the center of attention," was Deena's take on it. As the lyrics from James Taylor's song played, "I just want to stop and thank you baby," I whispered to my bride,

"Deena, How Sweet it is to be loved by you!"

CHAPTER SIX

*You are the sunshine of my life
That's why I'll always be around,
You are the apple of my eye,
Forever you'll stay in my heart.*

~Stevie Wonder

OUR FIRST FEW months of married life sped by quickly. Shortly after, we were *happily* greeted by the wonderful news that Deena was pregnant. I wanted to shout it from the rooftop. *My friends claim I did.* During the pregnancy, everyone in our family and our close friends were anxious to learn whether our future *Baby J* would be coming home in pink or blue. We chose not to know the gender until the birth. Our family claims that we *tortured* them with our refusal to find out the sex but we kept our resolve. The due date was September 5, 2006, although *Baby J* attempted to make an early arrival on July 27. Nearly a month later on August 23, after 12 hours of labor, our baby made its triumphant debut weighing in at a hefty 8 lbs, 8 oz, and 22 inches long. *Our precious bundle-of-joy was beautiful.* Instantly, we fell madly in love and could not wait to introduce the newest member of the Leider and Pizzichetta family to our loved ones.

Since this was going to be one of the most joyful announcements ever, Deena and I put much thought into the presentation. The one thing I was sure of, if it was a boy, I would announce my new business partner: *"Echo Valley and Son."* If it was a girl, I would shout out, *we just added another beautiful princess to the Leider family* and *Hail to the Queen in the Pizzichetta family.*

On that hot August day, I shouted, *Welcome Jason Jeffrey Leider/Echo Valley & Son! A baby boy, a son,* fulfilling all our hopes and dreams, entered our lives. His maternal and paternal grandparents were beyond excited since Jason Jeffrey is the first grandchild on Deena's side and *the first boy on mine!* The August heat was nothing compared to the warmth in our hearts. Enter, the *King of the Family!* Everyone was so excited to watch him grow, to assure his future be bright, and, for us, to be the best parents ever. As a father of a son, I thought about all the activities we would share. Not only would he one day become my business partner, but I hoped he would also become a football, baseball, basketball, wrestling, hunting, fishing, and four-wheel quad kind-a-guy. Lucky for me, Jason didn't disappoint—*he loves it all!*

The only temporary setback was that our little guy had to spend the first five days of his life in the Neonatal Intensive Care Unit (NICU) of Valley Hospital in Ridgewood, NJ. Jason had trouble breathing due to fluid on his immature lungs—a condition many newborns experience. Our son came home on August 27, 2006. Deena and I loved being parents and enjoyed our baby tremendously. So much so, that we couldn't wait to bring more *sunshine* into our contented home.

CHAPTER SEVEN

You are my sunshine,
My only sunshine, You make me happy,
When skies are grey.
You'll never know dear how much
I love you; please don't take my sunshine away.

~Johnny Cash

AFTER A FEW months of trying, we were delighted to find out there was going to be another addition to our family of three. Our second *Baby J* was due the end of February 2009. Again we decide not to know the sex of the baby until the birth. The excitement in our home was contagious. Jason was thrilled and told everyone *he* was having a baby and insisted—"Not mommy, *me!*" Jason's take-charge-attitude surfaced as he helped prepare for *Baby J 2*'s arrival. He even chose what Deena should bring to the hospital and what *his baby* should wear for the homecoming.

"It's another boy!" You can image how over-the-top I felt once again hearing those words. To our delight and immense happiness, Jason's brother *(excuse me, 'his baby')* arrived on February 25, 2009 at 5:23 pm. He was 8 lb, 9 oz, and 20.5 inches. Having delivered in only two hours, Justin Jay Leider was eager to join us, as we were to have him arrive. Deena and I were in *seventh heaven*, two boys—brothers, lifelong friends. Justin was as beautiful as his older brother. Similar to Jason, Justin spent the first week of his life in the NICU at Valley Hospital. Along with the difficulty he was having breathing, he was also experiencing tremors in his arms and legs. Thankfully, our baby recovered and was ready to join the family.

During a light snow shower, on March 2, 2009, we proudly brought our new infant home. We carried Justin into the house to join his anxiously awaiting *big brother*. This latest *little guy* was truly another gift, and the bond between him and his older brother was instantaneous. Jason was so cute around Justin. He acted like a "second daddy" by being helpful and super protective of "his baby." *We are truly blessed. Life is good!*

CHAPTER EIGHT

*Happy Holidays, Happy Holidays.
May the calendar keep bringing
Happy Holidays to you.
May all your wishes come true.*
~Bing Crosby

DEENA AND I always wanted a large family and having a third child was definitely on the Leider agenda. My wife felt we should wait a few years when Jason starts school. I agreed, but we both knew that achieving another pregnancy might not be easy a third time. We stored this "another-baby-idea" away for the time being and went about pleasantly enjoying our lives with our two wonderful sons.

Deena and I were your typical *new* parents. Holidays were always so special and filled with lots of excitement and fun. Deena and I could not wait to pick out the boys' Halloween costumes; go "Trick or Treating" with them; put turkey bibs on them for Thanksgiving; and decorate our Christmas tree with Jason and Justin's personalized holiday ornaments. We even shopped for the *perfect* Christmas Eve pajamas. At bedtime, we read their favorite Christmas books to them and, of course, on Christmas Eve we *left cookies out for Santa and carrots for the reindeer*. Christmas morning was fabulous watching the boys awed over their presents. Clearly, Deena and I were over the top during the holidays. The boys were also enjoying all of it too. As young as they were, we marveled at how *our enthusiasm and excitement* was passed on to

Jason and Justin. Our days were filled with laughter and love along with the anticipation of all the *great times ahead. We absolutely adored being parents!*

To our utter surprise and delight, we learned that *we* would be shopping for three Halloween costumes and adding a *third* children's ornament to our family Christmas tree. Our third *Baby J* was coming sooner than we expected. Deena and I were ecstatic! We decided to name the baby Jordan no matter what the sex. Again, we agreed not to find out the gender until the day the baby arrived. Once more, everyone had to be patient and wait for the debut of baby Jordan to find out whether it would be a girl or a boy. As our family grew, our plans and hopes for more *Happy Holidays* increased. *All our wishes were coming true!*

CHAPTER NINE

*Kindness is the language
which the deaf can
Hear and the blind can see.*

~Henry David Thoreau

DURING THIS PREGNANCY and shortly after Jason's fourth birthday, we decided to enroll him in nursery school. Deena and I thought it would be wise for Jason to be with children his own age. Unfortunately, it did not turn out to be as positive an experience as we had hoped. *Actually, it was a disaster.* After learning that Jason refused to interact with the other children and cried incessantly for his mother, we thought perhaps another school might be a better fit. A nursery school in a nearby town was our next choice.

The first failed experience prompted Deena to request that they place our son with the three-year old group. However, the director refused since Jason was four. At this time, Jason was experiencing minor health issues causing uncontrollable bowel movements, which made the transition to the new school even more difficult. As a result, whenever he violated the "potty rules," the school summoned someone to pick him up so they wouldn't have to clean up after these "accidents." To make matters worse Deena was on bed rest due to a difficult pregnancy and we relied on my mother to respond to the "urgent calls." The final straw was when Jason's grandmother was told upon arrival that he was "down the hall" in the bathroom. Much to her dismay, she found our timid-scared-embarrassed little boy sitting alone in a total mess. Jason was covered in feces from his shaking elbows to his tiny feet. After hearing this, my *enraged* wife called the school and gave them hell. *I went ballistic! Naturally, Jason never set foot in that damn place again.*

Locating a preschool for Jason with a good program and a nurturing philosophy was proving to be an impossible task. After countless calls to numerous nursery schools, our frustration was obvious since few met our financial needs and considerations. We wanted a pleasant, gentle, learning environment where Jason would acquire a positive attitude toward school as well as the social skills to facilitate interaction with other children. When we narrowed down a few selections, we went to visit them along with my mother. In the pouring rain, I carried a very pregnant Deena to the car and the three of us set out on the preschool hunt. My mother and I entered the school first because Deena needed to be off her feet as much as possible; however, she was brought in for the final stamp of approval. Finally, our quest ended successfully when we found a preschool with a quality program that met Jason's special needs and our goals for his future. *Kindness **is** the language all children understand and deserve!*

CHAPTER TEN

Is there ever any particular spot
where one can put one's finger
and say,
"It all began that day,
At such a time and such a place,
with such an incident?"

~Agatha Christie

IN OCTOBER 2010, Jason was registered at Nursery Rhymes Preschool in Saddle Brook, NJ. Since our son had difficulty before, we felt it would be prudent this time to *insi*st the school place him with the three-year old group. Although they honored our request, the transition still proved difficult for Jason who continued to have "separation anxiety." This was extremely upsetting for Deena and me. The professionals at the center assured us that this would pass and eventually Jason would come around and "adjust nicely."

Jason's behavior never improved despite our continuous collaboration with the preschool staff. Finally, in December, the director contacted us and requested that we have a private conference with her and Jason's teachers. At the meeting, Deena and I became fraught with despair as the professional staff cited their discouraging observations and analysis. Deena and I looked at each other with confusion and concern when his teacher uttered, "something just doesn't seem right." Jason's performance was below age-expected levels in academic, emotional, and social

A Walk in Our Shoes

areas. We were disheartened as we desperately tried to absorb all they were suggesting. When we finally regained our composure, Deena and I asked numerous questions and listened attentively to their valuable advice. They recommended that we contact our local school district's department of special education and submit a referral for Jason to be tested. As difficult as this was to hear, we respected their evaluation and began to put into motion the necessary arrangements to make sure that Jason's academic/social life be given all the available assistance he required and deserved. *Our ultimate goal was to help our little boy.*

Frankly, we already suspected some of the issues raised by Jason's preschool teachers. We did observe that he was both emotionally and socially immature in comparison to most children his age. When we would discuss it with our family and friends, everyone assured us *"not-to-worry."* We sought comfort in comments like; "My child is, or was, like that too;" "He'll do it when he's ready;" or "He has never been in school before just give him time." However, this time we listened to the teachers, even after these *well-meaning* friends told us "not to be too concerned."

Several months prior to Jason's pre-school issues, we had a similar situation occur with our family and friends regarding our younger son, Justin. Deena's "mommy-teacher instincts" kicked in when she noticed that Justin was not speaking at all. She had my complete support when she insisted (*actually demanded*) that we take fifteen-month old Justin to a speech therapist. Even at that time, our family and friends told us we were overreacting and that "Justin will talk when he's ready." They meant well and we appreciated their attempts to comfort us but we still chose to take action.

Contacting the right authorities for Jason was not as easy as we anticipated. We ran into several obstacles in attempting to schedule an appointment for an evaluation. When informed that the process could take many months, Deena and I realized we needed to help Jason *now*. An added problem was that health insurance didn't cover developmentally-delayed problems or evaluations. In addition, we wouldn't be eligible to receive services unless Jason was officially diagnosed with learning disabilities from the State of New Jersey. To make matters worse, we were put on a nine-month waiting list to schedule an appointment with developmental specialists. The delays, frustration, and overwhelming hurdles were numerous and endless. Trying to pinpoint the *actual* problem led to exasperating dead ends.

When Jason's preschool staff suggested potential signs of autism, we moved forward with this *possible* diagnosis. Our choice was a pediatric neurologist who attended to our second son Justin when he was two weeks old. This physician accepted our health insurance which facilitated scheduling an appointment. On December 22, 2010, we met with the neurologist, Dr. Judy Woo, for Jason. The doctor observed Jason while we answered the usual questions about medical and family history. Her medical evaluation was "Autistic-No, and Hyperactivity-Yes." Then she asked that earth-shattering question: "Did you take notice that he doesn't really look like either of you?" Deena and I looked at each other in utter confusion. Actually, we did wonder where he got that cute little nose, although many observers insisted he looked like "his daddy" (*I was proud*). Others even suggested that he resembled his paternal grandfather. Dr. Woo began pointing out Jason's atypical facial features, head shape, claw-like hands, and his extended belly. She also referenced back to Jason's medical history. Deena and I were greatly alarmed when Dr. Woo thought Jason had a form of the rare genetic disease Mucopolysaccharidosis but could not diagnose what form it was at this time. She highly suggested we see a geneticist.

The following day we received a call from our pediatrician, Dr. Howard Sonnenblick, explaining that Dr. Woo contacted him and they both decided it was imperative that we go to a genetic specialist. They referred us to a genetic team at Hackensack University Medical Center for January 18, 2011. After this call, Deena and I immediately realized that Jason's situation was serious. *It all began that day.*

It was two days before Christmas and we promised each other not to focus on Jason's medical issues. We avoided searching the Internet for information on Mucopolysaccharidosis and decided not to mention it to the family. Deena and I suffered in silence. *'Tis the Season to be Jolly—but not for everyone!*

CHAPTER ELEVEN

Pain and suffering,
The pain, the pain.
No birds are singing
Here comes Armageddon

~Iggy Pop

THE END OF the holiday season brought an end to normalcy in the Leider household. Our worst fears were realized when Jason was diagnosed with the rare and fatal genetic disease: Mucopolysaccharidosis-Hunter syndrome/MPS II. *Fear of the unknown engulfed us.* When the Chief of Genetics in Hackensack University Medical Center uttered, "there is no cure for it," the floor beneath me caved in and the air left my lungs taking with it my life's sustaining breath. *I thought I was going to die.* I turned and looked at my distraught wife whose entire body was trembling as she sobbed hysterically. I desperately wanted to wipe her tears away and tell her it would be *OK,* but I knew the lie wouldn't comfort either one of us. The intense agony we felt was beyond belief. Grief was swallowing us up—it was gut wrenching! *Where we ever got the strength to hold on at that moment still puzzles me? I had all I could do to remain sane. I felt our lives were officially and permanently over!!*

Little did we know that this was just the beginning of our inexorable pain, unending suffering, and indescribable despair. A few weeks later, to add to our anguish, we received the dreaded news that our two-year old son, Justin, also has Hunter syndrome/ MPS II. If all of this wasn't enough, my best friend and confidant, Kenny Adamo, suddenly passed away. He was my *go-to person;* someone I could always turn to in time of need. Kenny was a source of strength for me and now he was gone. With both sons diagnosed with an incurable illness and my best friend's premature death, I was feeling hopeless and defenseless. *How does one cope with such heartache?*

When Deena and I learned the symptoms and prognosis of our sons' heinous and fatal disease uncertainty, despondency, and extreme anxiety took over. This mysterious ailment literally eats away at its victims' organs, muscles, joints, and brain leaving its sufferers with a shortened life expectancy. Eventually, its victims are unable to walk, talk, eat, or recognize their family and surroundings. *This was the beginning of our sleepless nights and unthinkable thoughts filled with dread and terror of the unknown.*

A new year had just begun and instead of thinking about foolish resolutions, our thoughts were consumed by a terrifying reality. Our lives became inundated with doctors' visits, MRI's, and a multitude of blood tests. We were living the worst possible nightmare any parent could ever imagine.

The sense that I was losing control of my life was bearing down on me. My instinct to protect my sons was incredibly powerful; yet, I felt extremely helpless. Deena and I were constantly walking around in a mental and emotional fog; we were unmoored; floating around with no clear direction. I questioned how we were going to deal with this complex mysterious illness? We felt like a cruel trick was being played on us. Wrestling with our demons over this violent intruder became an immensely terrifying challenge. *It was sobering!* The birds were outside singing but we couldn't hear them—*the pain, oh the pain and suffering. Our whole world was falling apart!*

CHAPTER TWELVE

Faith consists in believing when
It's beyond the power of reason to believe.

~Voltaire

EVENTUALLY, THE ENTIRE family suffered from the impact of the disease that had befallen our children. Deena and I were in a state of utter panic. We were on an emotional roller coaster. Our whole world turned up-side-down, shattering our humble lives and our caring extended family. Deena knew how difficult it was going to be for me to inform my parents about Jason and Justin. They were so thrilled with their grandchildren I didn't know how to find the words to tell them both boys were stricken with a terminal disease. *It was incredibly difficult and painful to be in that unbearable position.*

To this day, that moment haunts me. When the words finally spilled from my lips, my father placed his head on the table and began to cry uncontrollably for his adored grandsons. My mother was inconsolable that "her baby's babies" were seriously ill and had to face physical pain and suffering. She could not accept the fact that their blessed lives would be cut short.

Adding to these desperate times was the death of my oldest brother Donnie, which occurred six weeks after learning the terrible news about my sons. Although my heart kept breaking, I realized I had no time to wallow in my grief. Remaining emotionally strong for my family was a necessity. This was the only way I could accomplish what I set out to do in Washington, DC.

Deena's family situation made it even more difficult for her to inform her parents about Jason and Justin. Her mother and father knew and experienced the agony of having a sick child. Deena's older brother and her only sibling, Matt, was born with a multitude of medical issues, which resulted in numerous and risky, invasive surgeries. Matt had to endure lengthy hospital stays in Manhattan at Columbia Presbyterian Hospital, some as long as three months. Their home became a mini-hospital when Matt was being treated as an outpatient. Deena was only a baby when this medical saga began but it lasted for eight long, difficult years. Consequently, she has vivid memories of its devastating impact on the family. Thank goodness, after years of suffering, her brother's medical issues were resolved (Matt did not have Hunter syndrome/MPS II). Deena felt horrible that her family has to suffer this again with their only daughter and her two little boys. Regrettably, they understand only too well what Deena is going through.

Jason was the first grandchild for Deena's parents and naturally was treated like a king. In due course, when Justin arrived on the scene he instantly bonded with his Grandma Lucille. To say both boys were special to the Pizzichetta family is an understatement. When Justin's *Nee Nee* Lucille is around, nothing else matters to him but her. Whenever Deena observes the incredible connection they have, she is overcome by the tragic situation. She laments, "How is this fair? My mom and I both having sick children!" "Why two generations?" "My mom and dad suffered with a sick child, and I suffered as a sibling having a sick older brother, as will our soon to be born child, Jordan." My distressed wife, demands to know, "Why me? Why do I have to grow up and also suffer a crisis even worse than my parents?" Although, Deena feels blessed and grateful that her parents still have Matt and she has her older brother, the thought of losing both her sons is too much to bear. *This cycle must be broken!*

Deena frequently and agonizingly calls out, "How much can one family take and why?" It was gut wrenching to hear her say: "How does one family get struck by lightning this many times?" She consistently questions, "Why don't I get the happy ending that I wish for others?" These probing thoughts make me feel incredibly powerless and insufficient especially since I am unable to respond positively. *What can I say? We just can't stop believing!*

CHAPTER THIRTEEN

There are two things I know for sure,
She was sent here from heaven
And she's daddy's little girl.
For butterfly kisses after bedtime prayer . . .
Little white flowers . . . all up in her hair.
~ Bob Carlisle

JASON AND JUSTIN'S unexpected illness blindsided us. A dark thick cloud became a permanent fixture over our once *happy, sun-filled home*. Deena was in her ninth month of pregnancy when faced with such inconceivable adversity—something no mother-to-be should have to endure. Since this disease usually affects males, and we did not know the gender of our soon-to-be third child, the morbid fear we experienced was indescribable and unbearable. With this disturbing news looming over us, everyone was even more restless to learn of the unborn baby's gender. Deena's anticipated joy was overwhelmed with uncertainty. Her sleepless nights became filled with dreadful thoughts that she might give birth to a third sick child.

Perhaps the baby sensed the nervous anticipation because, in less than an hour of labor, Jordon Kenna (Kenna named after my best friend Kenny) arrived. Our baby girl entered the world in the most exciting way. When the obstetrician announced, "It's a girl!" we were elated and extremely grateful. Tears of joy followed. In fact, the entire hospital maternity wing shared in our emotional reaction. Everyone began to cheer and applaud since they all knew if this baby was a boy he would probably be infected with Hunter syndrome/MPS II. *The applause and tears were abounding!*

Jordan Kenna arrived at 9:30 am, February 17, 2011. She weighed 7lb, 15 oz, and 19 inches long—a bit lighter than her brothers but equally as beautiful. Jordan is our newest *little angel* and, for Jason and Justin, a baby sister to love and adore. *Truly, this third, blessed child was given to us for a unique and very special purpose.*

Our newborn daughter brought enormous, much needed *joy* to the entire family. Jordan is an extremely pleasant baby who greets everyone with a smile and welcoming wide-open arms. In her frilly tutus and colorful hair ribbons, she is the polar opposite of her rambunctious brothers. She had to learn quickly how to handle herself during their playful roughhousing. Since Jason and Justin constantly confiscate her toys, Jordan learned quickly to share. Not by choice. *What they do share is their love for one another.*

Two *ordinary* people, who more than anything in the world wanted to raise a family together, were given blessed gifts—*three beautiful children.* We are thankful every day for our sons and daughter and pray daily for their happiness and well-being. Deena and I hope for future advances in medical research so that our sons will live longer lives. We wish for Jordan Kenna to grow up knowing and loving her brothers well beyond their childhood years. We yearn for the three of them to be an active, loving part of each other's future lives. Without-a-doubt, we truly understand and greatly appreciate why Jordan Kenna was given to us—for our profound love of children and for our home not to be childless. *One miracle entered our lives. Deena and I pray daily for two more.*

CHAPTER FOURTEEN

Courage is resistance to fear,
The mastery of fear,
Not absence of fear.

~Mark Twain

DEENA AND I were beyond elated to bring our *sweet* little girl home to her anxiously awaiting older brothers. Unfortunately, Jason and Justin's necessary medical appointments and procedures overshadowed Jordan's homecoming. Navigating through these unsettling disruptions with a new baby was difficult. We felt robbed of spending quality time with our bundle of joy. We were constantly shuffling her off to various loved ones while we met one medical specialist after another.

My wife and I were determined to understand every fact presented to us regarding the boys' illness. We also spent endless hours with our own independent research. Deena and I not only wanted to be the most informed parents, but we wanted to be able to explain to our concerned family and friends what life had in store for *the little boys* we all loved so dearly.

We learned quickly that there are various forms of MPS. Jason and Justin have the form identified as Hunter syndrome/MPS II. It is a genetic storage disease caused by the body's inability to produce specific enzymes used to break down and recycle materials in the cells. These missing enzymes prevent the proper recycling process in the body. As a result, cells do not perform properly and cause progressive damage throughout the nervous system; affecting the Hunter syndrome/MPS II patient's physical appearance, internal organs, and brain. This disease primarily affects boys and its symptoms typically develop between the ages of two and four. The average life expectancy of a Hunter syndrome/MPS II patient is ten-to-fifteen years of age. The only treatment for this form of the disease involves management of the symptoms and complications in the body—not the brain. The treatment is to keep it controllable; thereby, giving its victims some quality of life. *Deena and I desperately want to keep this insidious disease at bay.*

The more we wrapped our minds around this disease and researched, the more devastated we became. Getting up in the morning was nearly impossible. We just wanted to crawl back into bed and *dream this nightmare away.* The unbelievable notion that there will come a time when our two little boys will not even recognize us or their baby sister they adore was inconceivable. This dreadful thought infringed upon our every waking moment. The reality of Jason and Justin leaving this earth too soon left us in a state of pain we cannot truly describe. *As parents, we would do anything to trade places with them.*

Deena and I constantly searched for something positive with the Hunters' diagnosis but it never happened. *It just got worse!* We were forced to face the horrible reality that currently there is no cure for this lethal disease. We became frighteningly aware that insurmountable hurdles lay ahead for our *innocent* sons and us. My wife and I never imagined that something of this magnitude would ever enter our ordinary, normal lives and consume us with so much uncertainty and fear for our cherished sons. *Why does God make innocent children sick and allow them to die?*

CHAPTER FIFTEEN

So just kept breathing my friends.
Waiting for the man to choose;
Saying this ain't the day that it ends,
Cause there's no white light.
This ain't the end.
~George Michael

DEENA AND I feel fortunate that we were successful in compiling a brilliant and incredible medical team to guide us on this grueling voyage. Since Hunter syndrome/MPS II is so rare, with a mere 365 estimated cases in the United States and about 1,800 worldwide, there are few medical specialists versed in its varied forms. The boys' physicians quickly became extended members of our family. The medical team consisted of Dr. Hileo Pedro at Hackensack University Medical Center and Dr. Judy Woo, the Pediatric Neurologist who shed light on the whole situation. Others include Dr. Joseph Muenzer at the University of North Carolina Medical Center, the only MPS Specialist in the United States and Dr. Gregory Pastores, Enzyme Specialist at New York University Medical Center along with Dr. Barbara Burton, Clinical Geneticist at Ann and Robert H. Lurie Children's Hospital of Chicago.

Although we recognize how essential these doctors are to our sons' lives, the financial burden of these frequent medical visits, not to mention travel expenses, has become insurmountable. *How can our middle-class income support a family of five with these astronomical medical costs?* As I obsessed over this, I felt as if I were being strangled and as the noose around my neck tightened my anxiety increased. Our modest and carefree lifestyle changed drastically and as if the boys' health wasn't our only problem—now we needed to *count every penny*. I was terrified that we would lose it all—our house, cars, and my business. Clearly, Deena and I would give our very *last penny* if it would allow us one more day with our boys.

Even with this looming financial burden, my wife and I strive daily to search for the courage and unbridled spirit to conquer and destroy this *useless* enemy. As Winston Churchill remarked during World War II: "Never, never, never give up." With our incredible medical army, we will bravely soldier on. *This ain't the end! We constantly search for the white light to guide us. We will never, <u>ever</u> give up!*

CHAPTER SIXTEEN

If I can stop one Heart from breaking
I shall not live in vain.
If I can ease one Life the Aching
Or cool one Pain . . .
I shall not live in vain.
~Emily Dickinson

DEENA AND I discovered that in the State of New Jersey there are approximately five documented cases of Hunter syndrome/MPS II with Jason and Justin being two of them. Since Hunter syndrome is so rare, we were desperate to locate other MPS II families who could understand and share in this tragic situation. We were anxious to talk with other parents who could not only relate to what we were experiencing, but also shed light on what life is like for families affected by this disease. We searched for sources of solace, understanding, and support. We were delighted to discover the National MPS Society, a group that supports individuals and families affected with MPS and similar illnesses.

The National MPS Society is an amazing organization that exists to find cures for MPS related diseases. They do this through research, advocacy, and awareness. This organization provides much needed hope and support for affected individuals and their families. The Board of Directors is comprised of member-elected volunteers who are devoted to improving life for children with Hunter syndrome/MPS II. Deena and I were pleased to learn that the society also benefits from the expertise of a Scientific Advisory Board, comprised of excellent physicians, researchers, and medical professionals throughout the world. Their mission is to educate others about MPS and to raise money to support medical research and, therefore, promote longer, happier lives for those with MPS and related diseases.

The MPS Society enables the Hunter syndrome/MPS II families to contact each other and to share personal stories about their children and their lives. This camaraderie allows for much needed encouragement and support. The society also offers parents relevant information about new scientific advancements and research.

Deena, the boys, and I had the opportunity to attend the Annual National MPS Society's conference held in Boston. It was a privilege to meet all of our MPS families in person. The information we received and the companionship we gained fueled us to continue on this campaign for ourselves and all those we now call *"family."* We are eternally grateful for this wonderful organization for its efforts to improve our lives. Most importantly, we are *thankful* for the strong bonds we have developed with the other Hunter syndrome/MPS II families.

The National MPS Society's support and guidance has made it possible for families, including mine, to survive the trauma that MPS inflicts. It provides a therapeutic environment for us to share our emotions with others who are experiencing the same overwhelming challenges. This empowers us, gives us the strength to carry on, and ignites a fire in our bellies—to become *true champions*, underdogs who rise like those in *Chariots of Fire*. Our *ultimate goal is to strive for a future <u>without</u> Hunter syndrome/MPS II.*

CHAPTER SEVENTEEN

*A child must know that he or she is a miracle—
that since the beginning of the world there hasn't been,
and until the end of the world there will not be,
another child like him or her.*

~Pablo Casals

"YOU NEVER KNOW how strong you are until being strong is the only choice you have." This quote by an unknown author resonates since our strength has been tested by our sons' devastating prognosis. Suffering is part of life—this most of us accept, but a parent is not supposed to outlive his/her child, *let alone two children.* After learning about Hunter syndrome/MPS II, Deena and I had to find ways to deal with the shock and terror. No one can really understand the magnitude of the severity of stress knowing that your children are not going to be with you forever. The emotional and physical strain wears you down. We put on a happy face and do a lot of pretending; however, the special gift of our children's love is greater than any physical or emotional stress we encounter.

We know that we are fighting an uphill battle. The overwhelming magnitude of the management for their unusual ailment alone will be a monumental challenge. As dedicated and caring parents, we have no other option but to be strong for our sons and to make their limited lives as happy and *as pain free as humanly possible.* We work hard to treat Jason and Justin like typical, fun-loving kids. Being positive, and allowing our children to enjoy their lives, is our foremost priority.

Deena and I believe that our sons are very exceptional boys; *human angels*, who are put here on this earth to teach us all a special lesson. A very distinctive and spiritual lesson—*the fragility of life*. Our immense love for our children makes us celebrate the abundant gift our sons and daughter are to us—as are all children. We believe it is our destiny to search for meaning and we are eager to send out the message for all to receive. I plan to do just that in Washington, DC—share the lessons I have learned from my sons and this new-trying life we have inherited. Jason and Justin are *the miracles and inspiration in our lives*—there is an essential purpose and lesson to be learned from them.

CHAPTER EIGHTEEN

Always remember you're braver
than you believe,
Stronger than you seem and
Smarter than you think.
 ~Christopher Robin

ONE OF THE many lessons our sons continue to teach us is how brave they are as they face such grueling medical procedures. The most trying is the weekly four-to-five hour Enzyme Replacement Therapy (ERT) of the drug Elaprase. This costly enzyme intravenous treatment suppresses certain body organs from failing too soon. Elaprase is one of the world's most expensive drug starting at $3,285.00 per vile. We are currently at five per week; three for Jason and two for Justin—thank goodness, medical insurance covers this expense.

This drug is administered through a surgical implanted port injected into the chest. Deena and I are amazed at our sons' courage and bravery as they endure this procedure. In an effort to make things easier for the boys, my wife and I have had to be creative. Referring to Elaprase as "muscle juice" that will make them *big and strong* has definitely reduced some of the distress. The most endearing part to all of this is watching Jason and Justin comfort one another. Sharing the same ordeal has made the boys very close, but seeing both sons suffer is heart wrenching for Deena and me.

In addition to the medical procedures, we travel four-times-a-year to the University of North Carolina to meet with Dr. Joseph Muenzer, the leading MPS specialist of the world. He keeps us informed about the individual condition of each boy. We discuss their response to the treatment and the progression of the disease in each case. Dr. Muenzer explains about what is occurring in their current stage and alerts us about what will occur in the next phase. Every time we prepare for this trip, we pray we will receive positive news. Besides our trip to North Carolina, we must also travel twice a year to Chicago to see Dr. Barbara Burton, the genetic specialist. These medical trips are crucial in keeping the disease under control. We are also hopeful they will assist in slowing down the progression of this frightening condition.

"Midway upon the journey of our life, I found myself within a forest dark, for the straightforward pathway had been lost." These haunting words from Dante's Inferno remind me how easy it is to lose our way, especially when faced with seemingly insurmountable problems. Deena and I resolve not to get lost on this journey. We scrutinize and judge each problem, crisis, advancement, as necessary preparations to successfully continue on this meandering and punishing road. The exhausting medical pilgrimage that we are on is moving us further along the path in dealing with this unwanted trespasser. *Our shoes may get worn out, but we will persevere!*

Social scientists claim that pain stretches us to our limits, generally forcing us to look for guidance from others, and pushes us to consider new choices in our present situation. If we can remove the pain and heartache for our sons and others dealing with this tragedy, then Deena and I believe our lives have meaningful purpose. Helping others cope with the stress and trauma of Hunter syndrome/MPS II is our hope and desire. To reverse the course of this rare, life-threatening illness for all afflicted children is the force that drives us. My unwavering passion to help all these brave little heroes is the main reason I am traveling to DC. *This is a herculean challenge but I keep in mind that we are braver than we think!*

CHAPTER NINETEEN

A Little bit of sugar helps
The Medicine go Down,
The Medicine go Down,
The Medicine go Down.

~Mary Poppins

KEEPING UP a brave front can be incredibly difficult at times. For instance, it was a beautiful early spring morning, but I was unable to enjoy the day. I was taking my son Jason to the hospital for his seventh surgery. This time he was having carpal tunnel surgery on both wrists—one of the many debilitating effects of Hunter syndrome/MPS II. When we arrived at the hospital and the nurse handed him the required hospital gown, *my little man* refused to wear it. He protested: "Only girls wear dresses." (Even during the most difficult moments, Jason can always make us laugh). It's not easy for me to watch him go under anesthesia and have surgery. It killed me to see him so vulnerable and frightened. *It sucks, it just sucks! But it is not about me.* I held him and reassured him that he was *safe in daddy's arms and that I will never let him go*, as I always do with both boys during medical procedures.

Perhaps it doesn't mean a whole lot right now, but I'm hoping that when they no longer remember who I am, they *will* remember my protective arms holding them securely and lovingly—making them feel safe. *It's what a father is supposed to do* and it gives me satisfaction to know that I can comfort my sons. However, I never stop questioning, *why?* To gain strength, I pray to my brother Donnie and my friend Kenny and ask them to be with me today—*I miss you Donnie and Kenny. I know why you are up there, looking over us; it's for days like today. Please watch over my sons. Thank you guys!*

While the surgery was in progress, I headed outside to get some much needed fresh air to gain my composure. I looked up at the sky and my tear-filled eyes followed the clouds as they floated by. For a moment, I had the illusion of being carefree. *But that was impossible.* Maintaining the facade of a strong husband and father is becoming a challenge, nevertheless, *I need to hang in there.* Even the near-perfect weather annoyed me because I knew that poor Jason would be unable to play outdoors on such a nice day like other children his age.

After regaining my composure, I went back into the hospital and waited anxiously. The surgical procedure was successful but my *little* guy was now vomiting and miserable. I held his hand and whispered to him that *I will hold his hand forever and I will never let it go.* He cried, "I want to go home and lay on *my couch.*" Deena and I reassured him that he would be home tomorrow. We coaxed and tried to encourage him to eat a little but all he wanted was candy. Naturally, we indulged him with sweets hoping it would make his hospital stay a little less scary. *Making him happy was all we cared about.*

Jason was a happy-little-camper when we took him home the following morning, even though he was still in pain. My mood suddenly shifted and the lurking negativity resurfaced. I was deeply upset because having huge restrictive casts up to his elbows on both arms, my little slugger was unable to throw a ball, swing a bat, or even able to hold a cup, spoon or fork. More so, much to Jason's dismay, he could not even hold his ice cream cone, his favorite treat. Happily for him, *but not his parents*, Jason couldn't attend school. Watching him peer out the window at the other children doing normal things he could not do, deeply disturbed me. He was literally being robbed of his childhood. It hurt knowing that the complications of Hunter syndrome/MPS II will only get worse. *This is only the beginning*!

Deena and I were filled with relentless rage. While these emotions wreaked havoc on us, we made an effort to focus on channeling the anger into something constructive that would benefit our family. We knew it would not be easy but decided to "make lemonade out of lemons." Our primary objective was to provide a positive environment for Jason and Justin *just to be little!* To laugh, run, jump, and play. *Like all children deserve to do!*

CHAPTER TWENTY

It's astonishing in this world
How things don't turn
Out at all the way you expect them to!
~Agatha Christie

OUR SONS NOT only have to endure medical and surgical procedures they have to bear progressive physical and mental deterioration. When Jason's vision began to weaken, we were told he needed glasses. A simple excursion to the eye center resulted in a sad and trying experience. Choosing glasses wasn't the problem, in fact, Jason found a *cool* navy blue pair that unfortunately didn't fit—*they fell right off!* This was due to a physical manifestation of many Hunter syndrome children that results in a broad nose with a flattened bridge. We persevered and Jason continued to try on several pairs but so many slid off of his face. A relatively minor incident but nonetheless a frustrating one that made Jason sad and Deena teary eyed.

Frequently, Hunter syndrome/MPS II creeps up on us during life's most routine tasks and during simple moments. For instance on one beautiful spring evening, Jason and I went for ice cream. The sun just began to set as we walked back from the ice cream store. Holding and swinging hands, his tiny, soft hand firmly held on to my large, rough one. Happily strolling along, my little man and I quickly licked up the melting ice cream dripping down our cones. I found physical warmth from the withering sun beating on the back of my neck. Suddenly the warm feeling turned cold as my focus was caught by our two *quivering* shadows. I was immediately reminded of how fleeting life is—especially Jason's. *Is this what will be left of him—a shadow?*

A shadow of fear is forever lurking. It made my legs tremble beneath me. I felt as if someone had punched me in the stomach with a blow so powerful it knocked me down. I prayed for these depressing thoughts to go away. I pleaded to God: *Please, take me instead of my innocent sons!*

CHAPTER TWENTY-ONE

Let me tell thee, time is a very precious
Gift of God; so precious that it's only
Given to us moment by moment.

~Amelia Barr

THERE ARE MANY days we feel our lives have become a bad version of the TV show *Survivor*. It seems as if Deena and I are the only two contestants left on this primitive, unknown deserted island with no way off and all odds against us. As we continuously fight for our family's survival, we realize that time has become one of our greatest challenges and fiercest enemy. As parents with ill children, we are continuously racing to *beat the clock* that threatens to claim the lives of our two innocent little boys. We desperately want to stop the clock's constantly moving hands from robbing us of the many years we dreamed of spending time with them. Deena and I consistently hear life's time clock pounding in our heads morning, noon, and night controlling our very existence: Tick-tock, tick-tock, like a sick time bomb just waiting to explode. *The obsessive thought of "how much time do we have left with Jason and Justin" never leaves us.*

Our sons will have extremely complex medical lives—lives that will end between the ages of ten and fifteen years—leaving us broken hearted. These incomprehensible facts made us aware that life and time are transitory. Time feels like it is melting away right before us. It brings to mind Salvador Dali's famous painting, *The Persistence of a Memory,* of melting pocket watches. The life we once knew and embraced has become an instant memory, as well as the people we once were. Knowing two of your three children are living on borrowed time is too much to bear. *It is unimaginable and torturous!*

My wife and I consistently fear that our sons' lives are fleeting as we listen to the clock ticking away. We hear it on good days as well as bad. We hear it when we smile, when we cry, when we laugh, and when we pray. Like the immortal British symbol of time, *Big Ben,* which boldly and boomingly announces the hours passing; Deena and I hear it and fear it. It controls our existence—along with the harrowing, haunting, and excruciating question circling around in our heads, how can we stop the ceaselessly moving hands of time? *Time is running out!*

CHAPTER TWENTY-TWO

Old days, good times I remember.
Gold days, days I'll always treasure.
Funny faces, full of love and laughter.
Baseball cards, and birthdays.
Boyhood memories seen like yesterdays.
In my mind and in my heart to stay.
~Chicago

TIME HAS BECOME so many things for us now; with different meanings and purposes. Desperately trying to overcome this unbearable truth, we find solace when we choose to spend as much time with our children as we possibly can. Treasuring all the adorable things they say, and watching the priceless things they do. We beam when they smile and find absolute joy in their infectious laughter. Our intent is to create memories to keep and share with our daughter long after our precious sons have left us. The words life and time take on a new, special, and essential meaning—especially when you know it is limited. Deena and I had to quickly prioritize what is important to us. *We have no time to waste!*

Sadly, many of our days are spent running back and forth for medical testing, and doctors' appointments. Deena and I do our very best to keep our home as stress free and pleasant as possible. We make sure we give the boys the time for, "One more story before bed," even when we know it is past their bedtime and lights should be turned off. "Yes, you can sleep with us!" is our consistent response when they *beg and plead to come and sleep in our bed with us*. People say that time changes things, but I firmly believe you have to change and alter things yourself.

Keenly aware that time is not on our side, each night I kneel at my sons' bedside; cover them with a soft cuddly blanket, smother them with kisses, and wish them *good night and sweet dreams*, while holding back tears. There is a lump in my throat. I *cringe* and *mourn* knowing that these special moments are passing and I am one night closer to our final *goodbye*.

To maintain our sanity Deena and I concentrate on keeping ourselves from falling deeper into *paralyzing* despondency. We try hard to focus fully on our *living, breathing* sons and our amazing family. My wife and I embrace every special moment and promise never to allow time to erase the beautiful memories we have and will continue to create. *These memories will be all we have left.*

CHAPTER TWENTY-THREE

Memory is a way of holding
On to the things you love,
The things you are,
The things you never want to lose.
                         ~The Wonder Years

OBVIOUSLY THIS IS not the life we planned for our sons; but like other children their age we try to keep their lives brimming with cheerful activities. Deena and I *gladly* work hard at making every day special and fun for our children. The boys play and enjoy baseball, football and other sports. Jason loves to sit on the couch and watch TV programs such as *Dora and Diego*, and most preschool shows. Justin likes building things and watching YouTube videos on his iPad. Deena always remarks that she gets such a kick out of seeing Justin "build a stable house with his solid blocks." Like Justin, we work hard at building a strong family foundation for our children.

I get such a thrill when one of them sneaks out of bed at night, quietly tip toes down the squeaking stairs, jumps next to me on the couch, and snuggles in the warmth of my body. I place my strong protective arm around my boy and watch a *male* program on TV. Watching together, we gleefully and *greedily* share snacks. *Who cares about the crumbs!*

Many cute-simple things our children do bring smiles to our faces and make us extremely happy. Birthdays are a huge celebration in our families. When Deena's dad recently celebrated his birthday, it resembled an episode from *The Little Rascals*. It was so cute watching and listening to Jason sing the "Birthday Song" at the top of his lungs while anxiously waiting to help Grandpa Sal blow-out the candles. Justin, our *"little rat,"* strategically planned and connived to push his brother aside so *he could* blow out the candles first. Of course, Jason would not have it. He pushed his brother aside and tried to blow out the candles himself. A boxing match erupted but Grandma Lucille defused the situation by relighting the candles giving Justin his turn! *Happy Birthday, Grandpa Sal . . . from your Little Rascals*. Moments like these provide much needed laughter. *These precious and tender moments can never be taken away from us.*

CHAPTER TWENTY-FOUR

You make me smile like the sun.
Fall out of bed, sing like a bird.
Dizzy in my head.
You make me smile.

~Uncle Kracker

ONE OF MY favorite weekend rituals is when I try to spend Saturdays with my boys. I call it "*A Day with Daddy.*" We usually head down to our hometown Elmwood Park Recreation field and *hang* with some of my fellow coaches, sports dads, and Jason and Justin's teammates. Jason and Justin adore going there, running around with their friends, or just "hanging out." We spend enjoyable time with a group of fun-social people—*you know, these fanatic* sports dads.

Just like most families with little ones, fun times never pass without glitches and can become quite irksome. Every time I think about this one particular "Day with Daddy," I can't help but laugh now, however, at the time it took every ounce of me not to *lose it*. It was a day when we just arrived at the recreation field and Justin, at the top of his lungs, announces, "Daddy, I did poop in my pants." Frustrated, I yelled, "You did what?!" All of my friends and family know I keep my truck fastidiously clean, for that reason, I was *really* upset. Justin looked at me unfazed, and with his little baby voice, repeated, "I do poop in my pants." I cautiously and hesitantly took him out of the truck, and carefully put my finger near his diaper. Sure enough, *it* was oozing up out of his diaper

A Walk in Our Shoes

and all over him. I screamed, "Justin, you really *did* poop!" After a bit of hesitation, he sheepishly looked at me and whimpered, "I pooped." I shouted: *You sure did!* To deal with this unexpected and unwanted *messy* situation, I placed Jason back in the truck in the driver's seat. This made him exceedingly happy since he imagined he was a racecar driver. The Indies had nothing on my little speed demon in his actively creative mind. While Jason was driving the Indie 500, I changed Justin's stinky, super messy diaper. Being frustrated, I said to myself, *He couldn't do it five minutes early while we were at our house so his mother could change him?* A silly story, but this is typical in most families with young, *unpredictable* children. *Gotta Love My Boys!*

After spending time at the recreation field, we usually go for lunch at one of Jason and Justin's favorite hot dog spots, The River View East, also in Elmwood Park—a Jersey favorite. Everyone knows *my boys* there—they're like little celebrities. Our home town is an important, intricate part of our family and life. Some Saturdays, after we chow down, we go to the pet store to feed the fish, or to the ice cream and candy store; clearly every kids favorite place. Making Jason and Justin's smile and knowing they are happy is our mission. Our "Day with Daddy" is very special!

When Deena and Jordan come, it makes it a real "Family Day." In the fall we go apple picking. It is their Mommy's favorite fall activity. (If we are lucky, we might get a delicious apple pie). In winter, we build a gigantic, goofy looking snowman, make snow angels, and sometimes, even have an all out snowball fight. In the spring and summer the boys come to work with "daddy" or go down to the New Jersey shore where Jason and Justin chase after the seagulls followed by wobbly Jordan. They also love playing in the wet sand but know to clean up before getting into my truck. Jason, Justin and Jordan also build sand castles, search for a pirate's treasure, or sing about "Sponge Bob Square Pants," *who lives in a pineapple under the sea.* After the beach we take the kids on the boardwalk for rides and games and ice cream. We do this not only to bond with our children, but, more importantly, to create wonderful times and to escape the harsh reality of doctors and hospitals. *Whatever makes our children happy makes Deena and me very happy.*

Frequently we try to do simple activities as a family. Similar to most children their age, they love going to the park. They enjoy sliding down the slide, playing ball, maneuvering on the monkey bars or just running around chasing each other or after a furry creature. We frequent the firehouse where Jason and Justin proudly sit on the fire truck wearing the impressive huge firefighter's helmets—pretending they are driving off to a blazing fire where they will bravely put it out, rescue the people, and become "fire" heroes. We go to BWO "Body/Slam Wrestling Showdown" matches where we watch the likes of wrestler, Richie Rotten, and dance to "I'm Sexy and I Know it." In chorus, we hoot and holler, stomp our feet, jump up and yell "pin him down," and have a great time. This activity has been the inspiration of frequent spontaneous wrestling matches in our house. The wrestling ring being Jordan's "pack n play;" starring Muscle Mania Jason along with Mr. Hulk the Rat, Justin. *Surely, this is not Deena's favorite activity.*

Along with all that outdoor fun and craziness, Deena, the kids, and I adore having a leisurely *family night.* The children get into their *comfy* pajamas and lounge on the couch to watch our favorite movies. Deena makes a huge bowl of popcorn and we huddle under a large, cozy blanket laughing and howling at the TV. During the winter, we add hot chocolate with gooey, sweet miniature marshmallows to the menu.

The Polar Express is one of our family favorites even though it is a holiday movie. Although you can find us watching it on any given day of the year, we've made it a tradition to watch it on Christmas Eve. I recall the lines of Hero Boy: "On Christmas Eve many years ago I laid quietly in my bed. I did not rustle the sheets, I breathed slowly and silently. I was listening for a sound I was afraid I'd never hear; the sound of Santa's sleigh bells." *Remembering this, I pray my sons and daughter will always hear the joyful bells of Santa's sleigh.* While Deena is in the kitchen making us hot chocolate, the kids and I shout out to her, "Here we have only one rule, never, ever let it cool, keep it cooking in the pot, soon we got hot chocolate," mimicking the Conductor in *Polar Express*.

Another favorite movie is *Sandlot*. It is a wonderful baseball film for children and, given my sons' passion for sports, it is not surprising how much they love it. One of the greatest lines in the movie is from the character, Benny Rodriguez: "Man, this is baseball. You gotta stop thinking. Just have fun. I mean, if you were having fun you would've caught that ball." I want my children to always have a ball in life; catching the high ones and the low ones; and always having fun. Jordan also enjoys *Sandlot*. *She is definitely influenced by her daddy and older brothers. Play ball!*

Periodically, my avid sports enthusiasts will insist we watch a princess movie to please their little sister. This inevitably creates a big debate between the rivaling brothers over which princess movie to watch and who will play the part of the prince? Of course, Jordan always gets to be the princess whether it is Snow White, Cinderella, or Ariel. Cinderella is most befitting for my little girl since she is constantly missing a shoe and, like the fairytale, the siblings are the villains. Our mischievous boys love to hide and throw shoes behind random pieces of furniture and unfortunately, Jordan's shoes are often confiscated. The difference between the story of *Cinderella* and my two little princes is that the boys have learned that if they do not find the missing shoe and bestow it upon their princess sister quickly, the rest of their day or night may not have a *happy-ending*.

    Deena and I make every effort to create a sense of normality in our home. We strive to be the family we once were and dreamed of being before Hunter syndrome/MPS II attacked and destroyed our cozy existence. This cruel and unrelenting enemy took away the warmth and left an unbearable chill. Although it seems impossible that we could ever feel that comforting warmth again, we are determined to try. Often when we sit on the couch, wrapped in our blankets, the family photos adorning our walls, remind us of the special moments we've shared as a family. The key is to maintain that strong sense of family to enable us to withstand and resist the enemy as much as possible.

CHAPTER TWENTY-FIVE

*We must become the change
we wish to create.*

~Mahatma Gandhi

DEENA AND I will always embrace the comforts of our home and our fun-filled activities; however, we believe there is no place on this planet where we will ever find inner peace. The roller coaster of emotions wreaks havoc on our inner core taking us to the depths of the darkest abyss where we seek refuge. We continually try to find a way out of this bleak, dark place but we never seem to be very successful—we always end back there. I keep obsessing over the possibility that my boys will end up as mere shadows; whereas, Deena is consumed with questions about, "Why and how did this happen?"

Call me *morose* but there are times when I envision myself sitting front row at my son's funeral gazing teary-eyed at a *closed casket*. There are flowers everywhere emitting a powerful, sickening scent that permeates my nostrils and makes me nauseous. People are sobbing and wailing. Suddenly, I flash back to the moments when I see Jason getting off the school bus, smiling and calling "Daddy." Immediately after this image, his voice is silenced. The vision of my sons being buried consumes me. Wallowing in morbid thoughts is not healthy; similar to a dismal fog, they cloud the cheerful moments and leave a depressing atmosphere. Although it is an uphill battle to remain positive, I realize that the brooding *must stop!* I cannot allow feelings of hopelessness to take over my family's lives. If I must climb every insurmountable summit and scream out our horrific story in hopes of conquering this unwanted invader and saving my family, *I will do it! I just need to figure out how?*

CHAPTER TWENTY-SIX

Silently, one by one,
In the infinite meadows of heaven,
Blossomed the lovely stars,
The forget-me-nots of the angels.
~Henry Wadsworth Longfellow

THE EVENING WAS warm and peaceful. Outside a beautiful, star filled sky greeted me and as I looked up at the heavens, I immediately thought about my late brother Donnie and my best friend Kenny. *On an evening like this, Ken and I would most likely be sitting on the porch bull-shitting about the NFL, or about T-Bow going to the JETS (what a joke that is).*

My friend Ken Adamo's sudden death has left me with an unbearable ache and an incredible sense of loss and loneliness. Three months after Kenny's death, it seems inconceivable and unfair that I would also lose my oldest brother, Don. I remember thinking and pleading, *Donnie and Kenny, why did you leave me when I needed you most?*

To this day it is difficult for me to comprehend that I will never see them again, especially now with the struggles facing my family. I'm still haunted and filled with grief by my brother and friend's untimely deaths and learning about Jason and Justin's terminal illness. My struggle to come to terms with all of the misery has been ongoing. Grasping for inner peace, I found comfort in the *timelessness* of nightfall. I looked up at the brilliant night sky and gigantic mesmerizing moon, and suddenly I had this bolt of enlightenment overtake me—*an epiphany*! Immediately, *I knew what I had to do.*

If it meant reaching out to local government officials, various types of news media, banging *on the doors* of Capital Hill, and being a crusader for my sons, *I will do it!* Giving "rare" diseases their place amongst all the horrible diseases such as cancer, heart, diabetes, and others must be accomplished. Too many suffer alone, believing their medical conditions are incurable and their situations hopeless. *This will no longer be my position!* I am going into battle knowing that Kenny and Donnie will always be with me; guiding me and supporting me from above.

Neil Diamond's song, *Heartlight, speaks* to me: "Come back again, I want you to stay next time. A friend is someone you need but now that he has to go away, I still feel the words that he might say. Turn on your *heartlight,* let it shine wherever you go, let it make a happy glow for all the world to see." Miss *you guys—love you! You are my guiding lights!*

CHAPTER TWENTY-SEVEN

I must not fear.
Fear is the mind-killer.
Fear is the little-death that brings total obliteration.
I will face my fear.

~Frank Herbert

I REALIZED THAT with the genesis of my newfound inspiration I had to face my fears and fight—knowing that this will be the onset of a completely new set of challenges. First, I had to convince Deena that we needed to leave our protective shields behind, and expose our pain to all those who will listen. *How do I make Deena see that by keeping private we were giving in?* This was my first challenge! I had to persuade her that it would be OK for our boys if we put ourselves out there; become proactive, and start fighting for new research and more government funding. I felt keeping our story private was an admission of defeat and I was finished allowing Hunter syndrome/MPS II to be in control. I could not continue to stand by and let our stagnating suffering define us. *I was resolute that we will not let this heinous illness destroy our lives any longer.*

Deena and I began to discuss how we could make Jason and Justin's lives have meaning and a lasting purpose. Many creative and humane ideas started to come through family, friends, and our medical professionals. We gathered, and carefully considered all of these insightful ideas and opinions—constantly keeping Jason and

Justin in mind since *they* are the driving force that motivated us to implement this course of action.

The first thing I did was create a Facebook page. Deena created the narrative for our website to share our incredible story. These were the creative tools which helped us give exposure to our unique situation. Social media became the primary source for expanding our network about our sons' battle with Hunter syndrome/MPS II. Facebook and our website also became our daily means of communication. They enabled us to keep family and friends, who were inquiring about an update on our sons' condition, informed. It also allowed them to express their kindhearted thoughts and to offer assistance when needed.

Along with benevolent family and friends, Deena and I wrote copious emails and made phone call after phone call to various news, radio, and TV media. Our goal was to raise awareness about Hunter syndrome/MPS II. This dedication and endless hard work paid off. *We started to make enormous strides!*

Initially, we were a team of two but slowly people were coming forward to volunteer their services. On the night of April 11, 2011, we held our first fundraiser. It was held at the Venetian Catering Facility in Garfield, NJ. It was an amazing and emotional gala. Close to 900 people attended. We were blown away by the overwhelming turnout and support. The people who volunteered and attended this event were remarkable. Our astonishing and *numerous* family, friends, and newly-acquired supporters pushed us forward; held us up; and guided us this marvelous night. *Their love and support was earth shattering*!

During the event, we provided a video of our family's current lives, including some of the medical procedures the boys undergo.

To accompany this video, we chose the Lonestar song, "Let them be Little," keeping with our daily mantra of *letting our sons just be little*. That *miraculous night* was the kick-off and inspiration for the origin of Jason and Justin's trust fund and future foundation, "Let Them Be Little X2." The X2 represents the multiplication of 2 kids times their medical expenses, surgeries, medical trips, our heartaches and, of course, Jason and Justin—the special X2. The trust fund was set up to help finance the expenses for the boys' unexpected medical needs, to spread awareness, and to support research in hopes for a cure.

This amazing, angelic group of supporters joined hands with us—making us stronger and more resilient as we traversed this rugged terrain. In two short months, *this magical night, along with these incredible people, transformed it all.*

CHAPTER TWENTY-EIGHT

Family isn't always blood.
It's the people in your life who want you in theirs.
The ones who accept you for who you are.
The ones who would do anything to see you smile.
The ones who love you no matter what.
~www.spiritualthinking.com

THESE AMAZING PEOPLE and that life-altering night gave us new-found strength to build something greater than we could ever imagine. I'm a firm believer that "a house is only as strong as its foundation." A building cannot stand tall or withstand destructive assaults without a strong base and sturdy construction. "Let Them Be Little X2" is *our strong trust fund/foundation* made up of devoted, motivated, and selfless people. They reached out to us from various walks of life. Our common bond was Jason and Justin who deeply moved and touched them. Without these dedicated volunteers and friends *our house* would crumple. *We could not survive without them*!

These wonderful folks are essential and passionate members of our critical team that aid us with creating awareness and hosting our fundraising events. These fundraisers assist us in alleviating our medical travel expenses, medical needs not covered by insurance, and various supplies, which are needed to better care for our sons and their home treatments. They truly are our *community of newly devoted friends;* each bringing their own unique gifts and varied talents. These altruistic human beings have become our extended family. Jason and Justin have truly left an imprint on their hearts and have ignited an undying passion in them. They in turn, have given us the motivation and courage to: *Live for today, hope for tomorrow and never stop believing.*

These incredible people empower us; give us consistency, stability, and optimism. They add a booming volume to our once weak voices and give focused vision to our cause thus creating a broader-educated audience. Deena and I recognize our family, friends, and volunteers when we reflect on this sacred affirmation: *Isn't it amazing how God brings the right people into your life at the right time! People who support, love, and pray for you, regardless of your circumstances.* Deena and I needed a life preserver to keep us from drowning in sorrow and these people saved us by their supportive buoyancy. To these noteworthy souls, Deena and I will forever be indebted. Former Secretary of State Hillary Rodham Clinton's book, *It Takes a Village*, professes, "it takes a village" to support, sustain, and strengthen its children. I absolutely believe my family has been embraced by the model of what a perfect village/world should be. We applaud all those valiant souls who strive to make a difference in someone else's life. *Our family is truly blessed!*

CHAPTER TWENTY-NINE

Now cracks a noble heart.
Good-night sweet prince and flights
Of angels sing thee to thy rest.
~William Shakespeare

MY WIFE AND I never dreamed that one day our story would be on local and major TV networks. I always thought my moment on TV would be me, being spotted in the audience while attending a Dallas Cowboy game, doing a victory dance after a Cowboy Super Bowl win.

Looking back, the amount of progress we have achieved only eight weeks after the diagnosis is nothing short of amazing. By writing countless letters to newspapers and local and major TV networks, along with the help of Dr. Robert Tozzi, Chief of Pediatric Cardiology at Hackensack University Medical Center, we were able to share our story on Fox News. The connection to the news station came about when Dr. Tozzi approached his colleague, Dr. Manna Alvarez, Senior Managing Editor of the Fox 5 Health News, on our behalf. These physicians saw the uniqueness of our situation and stepped in to help. The rarity of Hunter syndrome/ MPS II along with the incredible fact that we have *two sons* afflicted with this disease has garnered attention. This program *gave* us a much needed platform and exposure in reaching a huge, broader audience. It not only put a spotlight on rare genetic diseases but also opened the way for other networks to profile our story.

In the TV show, *Human Factor*, CNN weekly profiles survivors who, the script reads, "have overcome the odds—confronting a life obstacle, injury, illness or other hardships." On September 6, 2011, Dr. Sanjay Gupta shared our distinctive story in the "*Human Factor*" segment entitled: "Family Vows to Live for Dying Boys." *It was devastating to hear the title.* The program started with Dr. Gupta sharing our exceptional story to the audience. He was so perceptive when he claimed that our family was able to tap "inner strength" and "resilience" something we "didn't even know" we "possessed." After this insightful introduction, he announced, "This week, meet the Leider family, who had it all and then faced the most trying of times, only to end up helping others during their grief."

Deena and I shared our personal life-altering story while Jason and Justin sat quietly. We discussed our marriage, the birth of our sons, and how normal our life was before our sons were stricken with the deadly disease. Our life's drama unfolded as we emphasized, "This was our perfect family. We were living out our dream, so we thought!" We revealed how in January 2011, Hunter syndrome/MPS II shattered our lives. When the gravity of our situation struck we wondered, "How could this be? How could both our boys have this fatal disease?" Undoubtedly, the most dramatic moment was when we expressed our worst fear and questioned, "How do we possibly even think of life without these little guys?" As the camera panned over to 4-year old Jason and 2-year old Justin, who looked so adorable in their NY Yankee shirts and hats, their innocence was magnified. Dr. Gupta explained that, "The worst is these parents having to sit back and wait for the days when Jason and Justin's brain and body parts deteriorate so significantly that they will lose all communication and the ability to walk." It was extremely difficult for us when we heard him say, "Most horrible they will not be able to recognize their surroundings and ultimately not know who their Mommy, Daddy, and baby sister are any more." Although we were aware of this, hearing it so blatantly *ripped opened our wounded hearts.* "Undeniably," I responded, "this waiting game has left our family's lives in complete and utter turmoil."

Since Human Factor is about survivors, it was a perfect forum for our cause. Once the gravity of the situation sunk in, Deena and I wanted to become proactive in combating the intruder. When Deena spontaneously uttered, "Why can't life just let them be little," she inadvertently set the stage for our future actions. Dr. Gupta explained how this plea manifested itself into our unique foundation: "Let Them Be Little X2." He praised the many incredible people involved and educated the audience about our passionate goal to raise awareness about rare genetic diseases and to work feverishly to find ways for pretesting and eventually, an ultimate cure. The community of persons at risk is fortunate to have the media spread the word about special medical programs that can assist in seeking and securing a cure for rare diseases. Our personal journey has benefited from this and we are now *on to new and hopeful horizons.*

The great American poet Ralph Waldo Emerson's words, "Do not go where the path may lead, go instead where there is no path and leave a trail." These insightful words encourage us to pave our own way as we continue on this life-saving journey.

CHAPTER THIRTY

Each warrior wants to leave the mark of his will,
His signature on important acts he touches.
This is not the voice of ego but of the human spirit,
Rising up and declaring that it has something to contribute to
The solution of the hardest problems, no matter how vexing!

~Pat Riley

AFTER OUR TELEVISION appearance, the outpouring of individuals, communities, religious groups, and corporations reaching out to us was extraordinary. It became a critical stepping stone for us to present our story to various organizations, local government officials, advocacy groups, academic institutions, and other special events.

One memorable event was when Jason and Justin were presented with the title "Elmwood Park Police Chiefs of the Day." It was extremely rewarding to see politicians and police officers give our boys their undivided attention. This was extra special since Elmwood Park is our hometown. It is also where we had the privilege to meet the Bergen County Sheriff.

Bergen County Sheriff Michael Saudino honored our boys for a special distinction. He made Jason honorary Bergen County Sheriff and Justin the honorary Undersheriff. Sheriff Saudino implemented this annual program to give special needs or ill children the opportunity to feel proud. These dedicated public servants have brought awareness to our cause and make our sons extremely happy. *Needless to say, the boys love every minute of these special occasions.*

The day the boys had their swearing in at the Sheriff's Department, I was asked to be a guest speaker. Apparently, others were also invited to speak, but I was the only one who accepted. Since there were approximately 400 people in attendance, I jumped at the opportunity to bring attention to Hunter syndrome/MPS II. I am indebted to Sheriff Saudino for his efforts in allowing me to deliver my message regularly at various events.

Raising awareness about rare genetic diseases, especially Hunter syndrome/MPS II, to as many people as possible is my goal. I believe this is the way to a future cure—*before it is too late.* I usually begin my speech by explaining to the audience that I am not as strong as I appear to be and through the immense struggle, Deena and I will never lose hope, never give up trying, and "never stop believing." Our story never fails to move those who hear it and their acceptance of us is always awe-inspiring, humbling, and motivating. There have been so many fantastic moments and fundraising events; way too many to describe in detail but all deserving of our sincere appreciation. People continue to join our crusade and offer us the opportunity to spread the word.

CHAPTER THIRTY-ONE

Hang on, hang on, hang on,
Little clownz,
You might just turn the world around.
Hang on, hang on, little clownz,
You might just turn the world around.
~Robert Downey, Jr.

ALONG WITH THE various events that have brought much-needed attention to our situation, we have shared many *private family pleasures*. One memorable occasion was when Deena and I took the boys to the Ringling Brother's Circus. First, I had to go to the bank to get more cash since Jason and Justin love to buy things and spend my money—*like their mother. A joke, just a joke!* Our *little clowns* felt right at home under the Big Top. They looked so cute with cotton candy smeared across their happy little faces. We bought bags of peanuts in hopes of feeding the elephants before the "Greatest Show on Earth" started.

Much to Jason and Justin's delight, there were lots of colorful, kooky clowns running around. The goofy-looking clowns raced up to the little children in the audience and placed funny, bright red, clown noses on them making the kids in the audience so excited. There is always a down side with Hunter syndrome/MPS II. When the red-nosed clowns approached Jason and Justin, and attempted to put funny noses on them, *they did not fit.* Here we were, at the circus, trying to be a typical family having fun when Hunter syndrome/MPS II reared its ugly head again just like the mythical Medusa. Thankfully, the boys were blissfully unaware, but I could see Deena's mood shift along with the pained look on her face. The sound of Jason and Justin's giggles and their loud shrieks quickly brought us back to a more joyful place. While watching the ferocious lions jump through hoops I was reminded of how far I would go to protect my family. *Hear me roar!!!!*

Although there are many great memorable events that blur the unhappy incidents, the *reality* is always with us. Without the generosity of local organizations, corporations, friends and neighbors, these cherished memories would not be possible. Like the time we went to see the Yankee's play at Yankee Stadium and were given complimentary tickets to see the famous Bronx Bombers *play ball.* Jason and Justin proudly sat in the dugout with all the players, and sat on many of the players' laps. *I know a few females who would have paid me to get that close to Jeter.* You can image how thrilled we all were. As a huge Yankee fan, I was more excited than my sons were—like a Jeter or A-Rod home run, I was *over the wall*!

This reminds me of a funny sports story which occurred on a perfect Saturday. I asked Jason what he wanted to do that day for fun. Excitedly he shouted, "Go to Cowboy Stadium to watch football." I explained, "That's in Texas, Jason, which is really far away." His innocent and sincere reply was, "So, let's get in the truck now and go!" Believe me, if it were only possible I would have gladly followed his command! *Gotta love my little MVPs!*

One of the grandest highlights and most fantastic trips the Leider family experienced was the one to the Magic Kingdom in

Disney World. We all became "kids at heart," and magically forgot about our troubles while vacationing there. These incredible times, make for lasting memories—memories we will treasure forever.

Something as simple as sharing a delicious family meal makes life tolerable. For instance, one warm night, I cooked a thick, juicy steak outside, along with my "infamous" coconut shrimp. *What a meal!* The kids screamed, "A Happy Meal"—they gave me a smirk when I teased and told them, *this chef is better than Ronald McDonald.* After eating heartily, we cleared the table. Deena washed the dishes (*remember, I did the cooking*). After we cleaned up, I gave huge bear hugs and lots of kisses to the kids. Deena received a warm peck-on-the cheek. These carefree times with my family are so special.

Activities with extended family are also very important to us. Jason and Justin love to run across the street to visit with my parents. My mother receives enormous pleasure cooking breakfast for her only grandsons. She gets such a kick out of their antics. After a hearty breakfast, the boys happily sit on the front porch with their grandparents, singing songs, and counting passing cars. Scribbling on the cement sidewalk with their colorful outdoor chalk is one of their favorite activities. Best of all, they love to blow bubbles and watch them float away, screaming excitedly when they burst. *If only I could place them in a bubble and keep them safe forever!*

The boys also adore going to Deena's parents' house—their other "super" grandma and grandpa. Deena's mother loves to have them over for dinner as much as possible and they *love going there.* Sleepovers at their warm, welcoming house are what

Helena C. Farrell and Geralyn A. Mancini

our sons look forward to the most, especially when grandma and grandpa come to say goodnight and smoother them with hugs and kisses. Jason and Justin are fortunate to be the recipients of so much love and devotion. *Our super family is the best!*

CHAPTER THIRTY-TWO

Crashing realities
exploding in imperfect landings.
Ouch; it's my heart that's breaking.
For these have been my fantasies and my world.
                              ~Mary Casey

O FTEN WE ARE not given what we want in life and being able to cope without a special talent or particular job is not impossible; however, dealing with unhealthy children who will not outlive their parents is. The natural instinct to survive has led me to do whatever is necessary for my family. For example, I never thought I would be adding to my job description public speaker, media spokesperson, and advocate in hopes of saving my boys' lives.

My family is eternally grateful for all the support we've received, but fighting the loneliness and despair is a constant battle. Having *two* terminally ill sons makes our plight truly exceptional. As Deena's husband and father of her children, I am the only one who can relate to this nightmare we're living. It tears-me-apart when she cries, "Only we can understand each other and the ultimate heartache we suffer every moment of every day." "We alone know how this feels." Her heart-wrenching, pathetic claims never fail to *unnerve* me because I know how *right she is*!

Deena was so proud that she gave me "the gift of two sons." She often says she'll never forget the look on my face during the delivery when the doctor announced, "It's a boy!" That same look resurfaced two-and a-half years later when we once again heard

"It's a boy!" I remember feeling so blessed because I actually had *two sons*—brothers. "We're going to have so much fun," I anticipated. There are so many plans and dreams I visualized sharing with my boys—sports, hunting, quads, working, men talk, and unbreakable bonding.

My wife fondly recalls how I continually thanked her for my children. *To this day, I'm thankful.* Sadly though, most days, "we don't feel joy." Deena loves to see how my sons and I bond, yet she tortures herself daily about the uncertainty of the future. "Jeff, you can never understand the burden I carry," she sadly divulges. Her torment intensified the day we learned that Hunter syndrome/ MPS II is transmitted from mother to the child; primarily to males. I assure her that it's not her fault, yet she finds no solace or comfort in my *honest* words. I am so proud of her; even with her conflicting thoughts, she braves on every day. She never reveals her suffering to her children. Victor Hugo's insightful comment, "No one knows like a woman how to say things which are at once gentle and deep," is an accurate description of my selfless, sensitive wife and caring mother.

When the genetic specialist explained that Hunter syndrome/ MPS II is an inherited disorder, Deena immediately felt responsible for transmitting the affected X gene to her beloved sons. Even the geneticist's assurance that no one could have known about such a rare mutation failed to mollify her. "A woman is supposed to be the nurturer and the caregiver, the teacher, the mommy and I feel responsible and helpless," she sobs. It tears-me-to-shreds when she accuses herself and cries out, "I can't believe that this is our life!" The most painful for me is when she uttered, "I died on the inside the day I found this out."

CHAPTER THIRTY-THREE

*You never know a man until
you understand things from his point of view,
until you climb into his skin
and walk around in it.*
~Harper Lee, *To Kill a Mockingbird*

WE AGONIZE EVERY day, as we watch the debilitating effects the disease has on our precious sons. Their health is constantly compromised due to the mental and physical deterioration they must suffer. They suffer from severe behavioral issues and sensory problems. The boys become extremely agitated, unruly, disagreeable, and, at times, intolerable. Their cognitive impairment and development lags affect their decision-making skills and their ability to understand right from wrong. It is extremely difficult for us to get them to do anything. They run from us and shout "No." Deena and I have to make up creative games just to convince (or trick) them to perform the simplest of tasks. The mandatory responsibilities on any given day are overwhelming. Jason and Justin's behavior magnifies stress levels for the entire family.

The boys wet the bed and subsequently cry out almost every night. We get up, clean them, change the sheets, and then try to get them to fall back to sleep again; robbing us of restorative sleep. Hence, in the morning, we are physically and mentally exhausted. The boys' attention span is zero; their hyperactivity is at the maximal level. Ordinary tasks, such as holding their toothbrush, spoons, are beyond their capabilities. In fact, they are unable to maintain their own personal hygiene. They cannot hold on to things for a long period of time. They are incapable of washing their own hands, showering and dressing themselves, and brushing their own teeth because their hands and joints are so stiff and their legs do not bend the way they should. To say they suffer from extreme frustration is an understatement. Being able to take care for themselves independently, will never be a possibility for our sons. This makes us terribly sad. Only those who *"Walk in our shoes"* will ever understand!

CHAPTER THIRTY-FOUR

I think a hero is an ordinary individual
Who finds strength to persevere
And endure in spite of
Overwhelming obstacles.
              ~Christopher Reeves

I WAS RAISED to believe that a man is expected to be the strength, the provider, the protector, the fixer, the role-model, and the loving husband, father, and, devoted son to his family. I feel inadequate at times and hate that I am unable to console and reassure my wife and parents, but mostly I lament over my inability to save my sons. My inner rage reminds me of *The Book of Job* when the devoted, God-fearing *Job*, who has endured so much pain and suffering, cries out, "Why Me, God?" When God responds, "Because I am God" the meaning is clear—human suffering is inexplicable. Like *Job*, Deena and I can't help but question our plight; however, the answer is beyond us so we try to remain strong and unwavering in our beliefs. Our silent, never-ending plea to *"Take this away from our sons"* is deafening.

Our devoted family and loyal friends are the ones we turn to for human comfort and support. Their enduring friendship is what gives us the strength to go on. Every day Deena and I comment how lucky and truly blessed we are to have them in our lives. The gift of these extraordinary people is the good that came out of the bad. The joy and privilege of meeting new friends exponentially grows. *Our friends continue to standby us and make our everyday struggles brighter.*

CHAPTER THIRTY-FIVE

Every step I'm taking. Every move I make feels
Lost with no direction. My faith is shaking
But I gotta keep trying
Gotta keep my head held up high
Keep on moving, keep climbing.
~Miley Cyrus

I'M NOT A renowned doctor or a brilliant scientist but a down-to-earth landscaper, yet, every day I'm fighting an enormous battle trying to heal and save my sons' lives. How does one cope with the knowledge that your two innocent, loving sons are going to die at a young age? *It is a terrifying thought!* It is emotionally exhausting and extremely draining but, as Deena and I constantly remind ourselves, "We will never give up or surrender—we will meet this challenge with determination and conviction." Our human spirit will rise above this nightmare. Our family will armor ourselves against the enemy who battles us daily. We will tie our shoes tighter and move on with confidence and with hopeful optimism.

Deena and I will continue to share our dilemma with politicians, news media, medical specialists, researchers—anyone who will listen. We will work endlessly to bring knowledge about this little-known disease. We will fight to change this unwanted fate and pray Jason and Justin's shortened lives will be extended. Our goal is to save them from this unconscionable destiny—including all those who are plagued with this insidious disease, Hunter syndrome/MPS II, and all other debilitating genetic diseases.

CHAPTER THIRTY-SIX

With a little perseverance you can get things done.
Without the blind adherence that has conquered some
And nobody wants to know you now
And nobody wants to show you how.
So if you're lost and on your own,
You can never surrender.

~Corey Hart

WHILE MY WIFE and I rigorously toil, we make a conscious effort to organize our efforts. Deena and I take on different roles. Recognizing that if we both did the same things, our life and family would fall apart. Deena describes my personal efforts this way, "Jeff is putting every ounce of energy he can into bringing awareness to this disease; helping our family live a memorable life all while struggling with the Food and Drug Administration and keeping abreast with research studies and trial medications." Deena is fully aware that my zeal is a form of survival.

Along with this, I try to be the best daddy, husband, son, friend, coach, landscaper, and a participant in running the house. My favorite role is to make the little ones *laugh—belly laugh*. Deena constantly claims that I am the real "little boy" in the Leider household. She loves to tell people how I'm always saying "silly, gross" things to the kids to make them *crack up*. In front of the boys, I tease Deena by telling her that *she smells like beef and cheese* while pretending that I am going to *gobble her up*. This makes the children howl and jiggle with laughter. I get such a kick out of seeing them laugh at every little silly, trivial thing I say and do.

In the mornings when I wake the boys, I mercilessly tickle them and goof around—Jason kids back by calling me "pickle breath, poopy pants, and potato chip ears" laughing until his sides hurt. Then he turns to his brother Justin and teasingly calls him "little meatball." Justin's innocent response is "I'm no meatball; I'm a little *RAT*!" We gave him that name, "Little Rat," since he is so sneaky. Justin has no clue as to why we call him *little rat* or what the meaning is behind it. We all laughed hysterically at Justin being offended at the "meatball" moniker, but proud of the "little rat" one. For example, Deena has a photo of our *little rat* Justin eating his baby sister, Jordan's Valentine chocolate base-ball mitt, which he stole from her. Does his *coined* name "little rat" fit his actions?

Deena and I allow our children the freedom to be themselves. She is right I'm the "real little boy" in the house since I instigate most of this silliness. I guess it is safe to say, I have always been "young-at-heart, a big kid that never wanted to grow up. I delight in being a fun-loving father and I believe my children benefit from it. I'm not sure my wife relishes the silly behavior, but every once in a while she does find me amusing.

Putting the laughs aside, Deena and I take our job as parents very seriously. With every ounce of her being, my wife dutifully keeps our family as "normal" as possible. Throughout this medical nightmare, her only wish is to protect and keep her babies as safe and "little" as possible. Deena strives to keep the fabric of our family tight and secure. She loves to play games with the children, watch movies together, and bake their favorite cookies; however, school work is a priority. She is responsible and successful in making our home a safe haven—*a happy place.*

While Deena prefers to be home, I soldier on and cope by being overly active and involved. I feel secure with the knowledge that I have my wife's ever-ending support. She arranges and keeps doctor's appointments and fights with obstinate insurance companies. Deena makes sure that we have an escape hatch in order to avoid MPS from taking over our lives. She accomplishes this by faithfully scheduling play dates, organizing parties, and social gatherings for family and friends. Her objective is to remove Hunter syndrome/MPS II from our lives as much possible while, at the same time, keeping it as close as possible in order for us to aid our sons.

Deena and I complement each other perfectly. While she claims that I am the "motivator who dives in head first to save the boys," she, in contrast, runs in the opposite direction. My wife does not want to embrace it or give it power over us. In order to keep her sanity, she simply wants to concentrate on making her children happy. Hunter syndrome/MPS II is frantically trying to destroy and take over our lives—Deena and I will not give it permission. As difficult as it is, we *will never surrender*!

CHAPTER THIRTY-SEVEN

*Books are the mirrors of
the soul.*

~Virginia Woolf

HUNTER SYNDROME/MPS II invaded our lives one year ago and the long and winding road we've traveled took us to a place where we wanted to share our story. The need to document our sons' lives and keep their memory alive was not the only driving factor to create our own book. Our goal is also to provide information and to heighten the knowledge of this unknown genetic disorder. We've made it our mission to contribute as much as possible to the conquest of this dreadful disease.

Our book is a way to fight back! We want this *book* to be written; we *needed this book to be written!* Deena and I will use *the book* to forge ahead. It is verification of our sons' courageous journey and for us—*it is a necessary catharsis.* At times, it seemed like we were narrating someone else's nightmare. "Can this all be true?" Yet this exploration has been absolutely necessary and crucial to our goal to do everything in our power to eradicate this disease.

A staggering situation such as ours will naturally rock even the healthiest and happiest marriages. If anyone were to *walk in our shoes,* they would fully understand the daily emotional, physical, financial burden, and marital stress we must endure. However, we fell in love with each other and that love is forever. Jason, Justin, and Jordan are three of the main reasons why our love *will* and *must survive.*

The Leider family continues to strive to be intact. *We will stay on track, get the word out, and most of all continue to be loving parents to our three incredible children and to one another.* Road blocks will deter us but this voyage will not be in vain. *On the Road Again. Bumps, potholes, detours and all!*

CHAPTER THIRTY-EIGHT

Let Them Be Little
Cause their only that way for awhile.
Give hope, Give them praise,
Give them strength every day.
Oh, Just Let Them Be Little.

~Lonestar

JASON, OUR SIX-YEAR-OLD, is super sensitive. He is a true *mush (Deena's choice of words)* who loves baseball, fire trucks, and being the "Man of the House." He often says he will be a good doctor and/or a popular racecar driver when he grows up. Meanwhile, three-year-old Justin is our energetic, busy boy who never sits still. He is constantly trying to figure out how things work, often with a devilish smirk on his cute little face. Deena labeled him our "push-the-button," feisty son. Justin also loves baseball and always has a bat and glove handy ready to play ball with anyone who is willing. His favorite pastime is pushing cars all around the house; maybe he'll be an engineer, a scientist, a racecar driver—*or so we thought!* Hunter syndrome/MPS II destroyed their future. As brothers, they can be as different as day-and-night yet their commonalities are their strong-bond and love—along with their fierce need to protect and comfort one another. For Deena, Jordan, and I they are the *sun, moon, and stars. Our children are our entire universe!*

Much to Deena's dismay, the boys love to play rough. Sports are a significant part of their recreational activities. As challenging and difficult as it can be for them, they participate in, or enjoy watching wrestling, soccer, hockey, basketball, football and, their favorite, baseball. Jason and Justin play on the Elmwood Park Little League T-Ball team and also Flag Football for the Elmwood Park Bombers. Their late "Uncle" Kenny is the reason for their obsession with sports.

Kenny was an ardent baseball fan and coach. From the time Jason could sit up, he instilled a love and passion for the sport in his little *surrogate nephew*. The two of them frequently played a throw and catch game. Kenny encouraged Jason to throw a ball in turn he would catch, fumble, and drop it, making Jason crack up and beg him to "do it again." Due to this constant routine of throwing and catching, Jason became accurate at throwing and hitting his target. *He hit it every time!* Kenny also taught Jason how to bat, along with Deena's assistance. At the young age of two, Jason was hitting a pitched ball. At three he was hitting with an aluminum bat. He slept in a baseball helmet while wearing his firefighter's jacket almost every night. *You think obsession is an accurate word?*

Naturally, Justin followed Jason's example. Deena and I tried to honor Uncle Kenny, after his passing, by teaching Justin baseball just the way he taught his older brother. We put markers on the bat where his little hands should be positioned and drew a batter's box with chalk so he knew where to stand and place his feet. Due to their condition, it is difficult for the boys to hold onto many items, so it was a huge accomplishment for them to hold a bat and ball. Sadly, my best friend left us right before Justin turned two; however, I believe "Uncle Kenny" is still influencing my boys' love of sports. "Take me out to the ball game, take me out to the crowd, buy me some peanuts and cracker jacks, I don't care if I ever get back . . ." *Play Ball! Gotta love my little sluggers!*

Apart from baseball, Jason and Justin's most recent playtime activity is riding four-wheeled motorized quads. Since the prevailing rule is that, "only big boys can own a quad" pacifier users were excluded. This required that their ubiquitous pacifiers be placed in the treasure chest at the "infamous" Lambert Castle in Paterson, NJ. Legend has it that this chest is guarded by a *ferocious dragon* and can never be opened again. *Goodbye, pacifiers!* This act of sheer bravery by Jason and Justin prompted the *noble prince* to deliver them a quad as a symbol of their becoming young men. *Meet the new princes of quads!!*

CHAPTER THIRTY-NINE

God has placed the genius of women
In their hearts,
Because the works of this genius
Are always works of love.

~de Lamartine

AT TIMES, OUR *human angels* reveal their horns and tails. One morning while playing a game on the iPad with Jason and Justin, Deena experienced this revelation. Each child was to have a turn but when Jason violated this rule, Justin became infuriated. The little one was so angry that he lost control and hit his older brother. Deena warned Justin that if he hit his brother again he would not be able to participate in the game. He then promised to behave but had difficulty following through with it. When Justin became frustrated and hit Jason a second time, Deena didn't hesitate to keep her word and barred him from playing. Oddly enough, this annoyed Jason who defended his brother and started to yell at her and accused Deena of being "so mean." He blatantly told her, "Say you're sorry!" Jason continued with repeated accusations to his mother, "You're fresh. You're mean!" To defuse the situation, Deena stopped the game entirely. Jason, usually the calm, quiet protector, began to sulk and weep. Contrary to this behavior, Justin was unaffected and cheerfully moved on to play with something else. Deena placed the iPad out of reach on the top shelf of a closet. Shortly thereafter, Justin nonchalantly walked past his mother with a stepstool. This conniving *little devil* brought the stool to the closet in an attempt to retrieve the iPad in defiance of his mother. When his short stature denied him success, his older, taller brother, stepped in and attempted to give him a lift. Deena immediately interrupted their antics and when she demanded they stop, Justin innocently asked, "What's wrong?" causing her to shake her head in disbelief. As she walked away, her inaudible remark that Justin was "such a scutch" was said with a smile. *Gotta love my boys!*

Deena's dedication and exemplary care of the boys never ceases to amaze me. She spends an enormous amount of time with the boys in the car transporting them to and from school, to medical appointments, and daily activities. She uses this time in the car to listen in to the boys' incessant chatter. She loves hearing Justin in the back seat singing and having a lively conversation with his TV character-friends (*Dora, The Mad Beast*, etc.), and especially with Jason. She informs me that "Their innocent babbling is like a chorus of youthful dialogue mixed with magical fantasy" and that she finds this to be "so cute." (*The little things in life make us smile*). My wife and I totally agree that Justin and Jason are definitely two very different kind of kids. With-out-a-doubt, when it comes to our boys and how great they are, *we are in absolute agreement.*

CHAPTER FORTY

Earth is a task garden;
Heaven is a playground.
~Gilbert K. Chesterton

THERE IS AN endearing story that Deena and I frequently revisit. It was the time when our inquisitive oldest child interrogated his mother about *Jesus and Heaven* while driving in the car. He questioned, "Who goes to heaven and what do they do there?" We believe this thought stemmed from the memory of Jason's beloved, maternal great—grandmother, GiGi. This moving moment greatly touched Deena with conflicting emotions. Her explanation was simple, "When heaven needs a job to be done, God calls a special person that He believes can do it." She further explained, "Heaven needed blankets so God called great-grandma GiGi to come up and crochet the most beautiful blankets for everyone there." Jason then proceeded to ask, "Mommy, what job do you think God will ask me to do in heaven?" Trying to keep her composure Deena replied, "What job would you like to do?" Without missing a beat, he said, "When I go to heaven I want my job to be to start my own baseball team and everyone in heaven can play on my team." Justin, joining the conversation at this point, shouted out, "When I go to heaven I am not playing on your team, because my job in heaven will be to start my own football team. My team will have the same colors as the Dallas Cowboys and we will always beat the Giants!" Deena reassured the boys that both of their jobs will be wonderful and that it will be such a fun, happy place. While this exchange with her boys was heartbreaking for Deena, it also served as a source of comfort. She hopes that when the disease takes over, our boys will have visions of the next life being a joyful, safe, and wonderful place where they will never become incapacitated. *My wife truly exemplifies the meaning of a mother's strength, insight, and love.*

CHAPTER FORTY-ONE

When you wish upon a star
Makes no difference who you are
Anything your heart desires will come to you!

~Walt Disney

OFTEN YOU HEAR people talk about what they want to accomplish before their time on earth is over—before they "kick the bucket." Some *bucket lists* may include a burning desire to climb Mt. Everest, run a marathon, or perhaps write a best seller. Others may wish to travel to an exotic destination or paint a famous portrait before their life ends. Still there are those who would want to score a winning goal or touchdown, or simply to find their one true love or soul mate. For our son Jason there is no doubt that he would wish for the opportunity to run with the cowboys—the Dallas Cowboys, that is!

Truly one of the most *bittersweet* moments for Deena and I since this journey began occurred when we received a call from the Make-A-Wish Foundation. The primary goal of this organization is to grant the wishes of children with life-threatening medical conditions as a source of hope, strength, and joy. They are able to achieve this through referrals and medical eligibility. Of course, no parent wants their child to qualify for this kind of service. Yet, the magic they bring into the world of medically challenged families makes you believe anything is possible.

Jason's immediate response when asked what wish he would want granted was delivered without missing a beat. He blurted out, "I want to go to Dallas Cowboy Stadium and run through the Cowboy's tunnel on to the field and hear my name really loud." Frequently, we would imitate and play this game with the boys at home. In a loud announcer's voice, I would call out their names and the boys would run through the kitchen into our living room pretending they were taking the field at a Dallas Cowboys football game.

I could barely contain my emotions thinking my son shared the same hopes and dreams that I had as a boy—*to play for America's team*, the Dallas Cowboys! The excitement in the room was contagious as everyone began to shout with glee. Justin, well aware he would be sharing in his brother's glory, started to run around the house screaming with delight. Jordan also joined in the merriment and began chasing her brothers around the room. This moment will forever be etched in Deena and my hearts for so many reasons.

Once the arrangements were confirmed, and the infamous day arrived, the entire Leider family, including both sets of grandparents, piled into the Make-A-Wish limo for the ride of a lifetime. The ceiling inside the limo was adorned with sparkling illuminating stars but not nearly as bright as the twinkle in my three children's eyes. The Make-A-Wish Foundation left no detail unturned including a snack bar abundantly filled with all of our favorite treats. We all felt like little children on Christmas morning.

Upon arriving at the hotel, they had greeters, gift bags, and posters in the lobby to welcome the *Dallas Cowboys newest captain, Jason Leider*. We were so astonished and filled with emotion, especially when we looked over to "Captain Jason" and saw he was beaming from ear to ear. Once Jason finished greeting his newfound adoring fans, we headed to our room. Our little *cowboy* needed to rest since he had to be at the field for team practice the following day. The next morning, Jason flew out the door as if he were on the gridiron running to make the winning touchdown.

Jason's excitement was palpable as we pulled up to the elaborate, massive—Cowboys Stadium. He was in awe to be finally at the home of his beloved team. A member of the team's staff greeted and then guided us to the Cowboys locker-room. It was so thrilling (I felt my knees go weak) to see the players greet their *new captain* and gather around him as if he were giving them a Super Bowl victory speech.

Our emotionally charged family stood on the sidelines as Jason's moment came to take to the field. He ran through that tunnel with all of his might as his name, "Captain Jason Leider," reverberating through the stadium. *None of us will ever forget that moment!*

The Dallas Cowboys played their longtime rivals, the NY Giants, that day. Unfortunately, they lost but the Cowboys will always be winners in our eyes and continue to be our number one team. After this unique once-in-a-life-time experience, we absolutely believe *there is power in a wish and dreams do come true!* "Captain Jason" absolutely agrees and never stops talking about it!

CHAPTER FORTY-TWO

*May you never take one single breathe for granted,
Promise me that you will give faith a fighting chance,
and when you get the choice to sit it out or dance,
I hope you dance . . . I hope you dance.*

~Lee Ann Womack

OUR EMOTIONS GO up and down on a daily basis. Gaining control is difficult because we live with overwhelming uncertainty every single day. This one particular morning, a seemingly typical routine Saturday, we were preparing to get ready for a baseball game, when Deena came down the stairs with red teary eyes. She just experienced an unnerving moment with Jason. While blow-drying her hair, Jason came into the room and bombarded his mother with a slew of questions. After chatting a while, he took her brush, combed his hair, and stated, "Mommy, I'm handsome now, like a Prince and Mommy, you're my princess." Deena smiled and answered, "Why thank you my handsome prince." Her little *mush* held out his hand and asked her to dance. The stark reality that she would never have the opportunity to dance with either of her sons at their weddings brought her to tears. While Jason delighted in dancing with his mother, Deena was "dying on the inside." Not wanting to upset the moment, she hid her tears and gently kissed her son as she uttered the words, "I love you so much!" Her eyes welled up again when he responded, "I love you more."

Hunter syndrome/MPS II controls the roller coaster of emotions we must endure. Disrupting a sweet, tender moment between a mother and son is a perfect example of its power. These setbacks throw us off balance but focusing on the positive helps us to recover. *We will never sit out a dance. We will forever dance with our children and give life a fighting chance!*

CHAPTER FORTY-THREE

*Somewhere over the rainbow, skies are blue
And the dreams that you dare to dream, really do
come true.
Someday I'll wish upon a star
and wake up where the clouds are far behind me.
Where troubles melt like lemon drops . . .
Some Where over the rainbow . . .*
~Judy Garland

IN ESSENCE, DEENA and I are dedicated to providing a happy childhood for our boys. We also are committed to helping others cope with the traumatic experience of life-threatening illnesses. As parents and advocates, we will work endlessly to assist in any way possible to render Hunter syndrome/MPS II a thing of the past.

I hope that no one will ever feel that we are exploiting our sons. As loving, protective parents, we will immediately put an end to any or all activities that are detrimental to our boys' mental and physical well-being. Their best interest is always foremost in our minds and hearts. So far, they have accepted the love and attention from hundreds of well-intentioned people with much enthusiasm. As long as they are smiling, giggling, and having fun, we will continue to allow their active participation in this *continuing journey. May their lives be filled with beautiful dreams and bright, colorful rainbows.*

Our motto is "Let Them Be Little"—*Ordinary lives for Extraordinary Children.* We strive to live in the present and acknowledge that life is fleeting. Our family must and will focus on the now and all precious moments we are given. The frequently used AA mantra: "One day at a time," is not a cliché but a formula for survival and sanity. More than ever, we know and appreciate this truism. But for us, most of the time, it is *one minute at a time, one moment at a time, one breath at a time*!

Ralph Waldo Emerson's inspirational words: "Do not go where the path may lead go instead where there is no path and leave a trail," defines our destiny. Through the pain and suffering of our family we are motivated to lead the cause to obliterate Hunter syndrome/MPS II. We encourage all to *walk along with us on this journey.*

CHAPTER FORTY-FOUR

You'll stumble in my footsteps,
Keep the same appointments I kept,
If you try walking in my shoes
If you try walking in my shoes
~Depeche Mode

SINCE THIS DIFFICULT journey began, our cumbersome shoes have become soiled, muddied, ripped and torn, but they still remain our sturdy companion as we continue to walk this rugged and rocky path. Along the way, opportunities to spread the word about our plight have arisen. One such instance occurred when a local news station invited me to discuss my family's personal experience with a rare genetic disease. This was a major turning point for us.

This TV program opened the way for me to connect with members of the National Organization for Rare Disorders (RARE). This organization grew out of an "informal coalition" of support groups and families called together in 1982 to advocate legislation supporting the development of orphan drugs, or drugs for treating rare diseases. This remarkable group succeeded in getting the United States Congress to pass the Orphan Drug Act (ODA) in early 1983. Members of RARE, who happened to view the TV show, contacted me and told me how impressed they were with my determination to raise awareness about rare diseases.

RARE members yearly attend an annual national conference in Washington DC, which promotes legislative advocacy for rare diseases. I was humbled and honored that they invited me to attend with them. This gave validation to our cause. The idea that I would be going to Capitol Hill, not as a tourist, but as an advocate, was mind-boggling not to mention awe inspiring. I was determined to leave my footprints from our hometown to Washington, DC, or wherever they take me, in hopes of making a permanent difference.

CHAPTER FORTY-FIVE

Born in the U.S.A.
I was born in the U.S.A!
I'm a long gone daddy in the U.S.A.
Born in the U.S.A.
I'm a cool rocky daddy in the U.S.A
~Bruce Springsteen

THE RADIO IS blasting in my *trusty* white pick-up truck. Jason and Justin's handprints, along with bold purple lettering of "Let Them Be Little X2," are printed across the entire body and proudly decorate the hood. I am traveling with my friend Jim Monaco, who is one of the biggest advocates for Let Them Be Little X2 and a special friend to our sons. We are driving on the New Jersey Turnpike to Washington, DC. With windows wide open, the unpleasant odor filling the air gives credence to the stereotype that New Jersey smells bad. Most likely, this trip would also have included my patriotic/history loving brother Donnie and my late friend Kenny (who we teased was my second wife) had they not passed away. Kenny's powerful arms would have lifted me up and carried me on his broad shoulders. Jimmy has become my *new* strength offering me invaluable support. Undoubtedly, Kenny is riding along with us. I can hear him joking with me that Jimmy is the cause of the horrendous "passing" smell. *I think he's right! I have no doubt these guys are in this truck supporting me and my sons on this journey.*

When Jimmy and I pulled up to the hotel in DC, I was awestruck by the sight of the historical monuments in the distance. We were in DC to attend the Rare Disease Legislative Advocate Conference (RDLA), which is also known as the Lobby Day for Rare Diseases. The RDLA is an international/global community created to empower, unify, and raise awareness for those battling rare diseases. This conference enables its advocates to discuss fund innovations and equips its members with new medical research information. It also provides a forum for voices to be heard. *And trust me, I will not leave until mine is heard loud and clear!*

It also affords its community the opportunity to meet and engage with scores of amazing people from all over the United States. Unfortunately, it is still a marginalized and isolated society that shares a common thread—the difficult task of raising awareness and funds for rare genetic diseases. We advocates are varied in color and kind, gathering to support the next new crop of *uncertain* members. We find support in sharing our stories filled with pain and suffering; however, we find the time for much needed humor. As Golda Meir, first female Prime Minister of Israel, so wisely stated, "Those who do not know how to weep with their whole heart don't know how to laugh either." In between the tears, laughter is good medicine. *I search for a little humor with each new day.*

At the RDLA conference, one of the most important objectives our diverse population comes away with is the realization that we are not alone. This makes it imperative that we continue on this journey together as there is "power in numbers." The intense battle we are fighting is draining us of the strength to encounter future ones; however, we will persevere. I, personally, am kept alive by the fire in my soul for those I deeply love and by my unrelenting desire to protect them no matter what it takes. Some of my friends think I'm amazing, but I don't see this. For me: *It's a privilege*!

CHAPTER FORTY-SIX

Oh, why you look so sad?
Tears are in your eyes.
Come on and come to me now.
Don't be ashamed to cry.
Let me see you through
Cause I've seen the dark side too.
I'll Stand by you, I'll Stand by you.
                                   ~Pretenders

A S WE ARRIVED in DC, my ambiguous emotions were restless, like shocking electricity going through my entire body, yet I am confident—*I have to be!* This might be my only opportunity to be heard by the powers that can determine the future of all those inflicted with a rare genetic disease, including the loves of my life.

While en route we received numerous texts from our "Let Them Be Little X2" friends—friends that have become my army, joining forces to assist me in the greatest combat of my life. Many other advocates of "Let Them Be Little X2" were texting us throughout our trip, offering their words of encouragement and support. These uplifting texts are further confirmation that we are not alone on this difficult journey. Their enduring friendships mean so much. *I was thunderstruck* with the outpouring of support. Words were inadequate to describe my feelings—and *that's an odd occurrence for someone like me.*

As we were driving through DC, I was filled with immense pride in our country. The thought that a simple man like me would soon walk the very same halls of Congress that great American leaders once walked amazed me. When we arrived at our hotel the valet insisted we put the truck (*my baby*) in the garage. I was fuming: *F—kin No Way am I going to let them shove and hide my truck; my armor tank that is a tattoo image, a true reflection of my objective in that garage*! Immediately I pulled out a twenty, slipped it into the guy's hand, and next thing you know, *the truck is front and center to be seen by all!*

I called Deena, and told her of our truck escapade. She laughed and coyly remarked, "Typical Jersey guys." When we returned that night, Jimmy and I noticed that the truck was not in front of the hotel, needless to say, I flipped out. Jimmy, holding me back and trying to calm me said, "Don't worry they probably tucked it away for the night." Frustrated, I rushed over to the valet and shouted, "Where the hell is my truck?" Exactly as Jimmy surmised, the guy's response was that he put it away for the night. The following morning we went to the entrance of the hotel and there it was—*my protective shield*, right in front for all to witness, "Let Them Be Little X2," handprints and all. *I'll stand by you, sons, I'll stand by you.*

CHAPTER FORTY-SEVEN

Children are surely one of God's greatest gifts
and truest challenges.
To share your life with a child is to humble yourself
so that you may learn from them
And discover with them the beautiful secrets
That are only uncovered in searching.
                              ~Kathleen Tierney Crilly

WAKING UP TO an encouraging, loving text from Deena: "Good luck today," gave me the momentum I needed to attend this conference and pursue our mission. Deena decided to stay home to care for Jason, Justin and Jordan, anxiously awaiting a phone call or text with any information about my progress. Deena would have joined me but she decided to remain home to avoid disrupting the children's routine—*I agreed wholeheartedly.*

A huge-broad smile spread across my face as I thought about what occurred with Jason the night before I left for DC. I told him I was going away for a few days to go into battle for them—my sons *love when I act like a superhero.* I instructed Jason to be "the man of the house" and that it was his "responsibility to take care of his mother, Justin, and Jordon." Jason likes being his younger siblings' protector and at times, their boss. He is a doting "big brother." He insisted that they're "his babies." When Jason was two-and a half he would yell, "Hurry up mommy, my baby needs you," as soon as Justin awoke. To this day, if they get hurt, Jason hugs and comforts them, often with words, "It's ok, I'm here." If Jordan falls, Jason runs to her and gently rubs her sore little head soothing her with, "no cry baby," or calls out, "help, mommy, sista cryin." Jason is a super brother and great role model. His approach is similar with our two little dogs, Boomer and Milo. Once when a strange dog attacked Boomer, Jason immediately ran to pet and console him, "It's OK, I no let anything happen to you!" *Jason protects all!*

On this night, when I told the boys that it was time for bed, Jason proudly responded in his five-year old chatter, "Ok daddy, you're the boss for now, but tomorrow, *I in charge*." He insisted, "I say when we go to bed and when to shut off the TV because, *I in charge!*" These typical, comical remarks by Jason, along with Deena's good luck text, sustained and encouraged me to carry on. I drove away my fears and uncertainties about the future, jumped in the shower, shaved, and dressed to get ready to face our Nation's Congress. Pumping myself up by exclaiming: *Here we Go! Jason and Justin, Daddy is going into battle for you!*

CHAPTER FORTY-EIGHT

Human progress is neither automatic
Nor inevitable.
Every step towards the goal of justice
Requires sacrifice and struggle;
The tireless exertions and passionate concern
Of dedicated individuals.
~Martin Luther King, Jr.

JIMMY AND I discussed whether it was necessary to wear a suit and tie to the workshop held in a formal conference room near The Capital. *Freaking* Jimmy convinced me that it won't be required. He boastfully said, "We should proudly wear our black "Let Them Be Little" sweatshirts, jeans, and sneakers." Against my better judgment, I followed his advice. I told him that if we arrived there and the other attendees were wearing suits, I would be livid. When we entered the conference room in our "proud casual attire," we noticed a few professionally dressed people. Unfortunately for Jimmy, as the lawyers, medical bio-techs, and important organizational *big shots* started to take their places around the huge conference table, it became evident that we were the only two not wearing suits. Jimmy, sitting behind me, looked around the table, cautiously wheeled his chair up to mine and had the gall to whisper in my ear, "Hey, Jeff, we should've worn suits and ties." It was difficult for me to restrain myself but I had no problem hurling a few expletives in his ear. In truth, I wasn't really worried about the fashion *faux pas*. *My main concern was my family.*

The focus of the workshop was to discuss innovative new drugs and potential genetic testing. Other issues brought up were the huge systematic obstacles and hurdles faced by those dealing with unreasonable roadblocks from the US government and the Food and Drug Administration. Various bio-techs and scientists expressed their frustrations in dealing with the stifling bureaucracy. The panel urged adamant and assertive action to promote this worthy and necessary cause. *We must be hardcore activists! We will not settle until funding for drugs, which alleviate and manage rare genetic diseases, are available.* Also, it is imperative that prenatal testing become a reality. *Trust me, my voice will be heard for all. I will not accept anything less!*

During this February, 2012, 3-day RDLA Conference, Jimmy and I also attended the Second Annual RDLA Cocktail Reception, Movie Screening, and Panel Discussion held at the West End Cinema in DC. *This time we followed my great fashion sense and wore suits and ties.* It was an incredible opportunity to rub shoulders with Members of Congress and with two-time Academy Award Winner filmmaker, Barbara Kopple. She is head of Cabin Creek Films and director of documentaries, narrative TV, and film. Kopple is renowned for producing documentaries that focus on critical social issues.

Kopple's most recent project is the documentary, "A Fight to Live." As stated in the film: "In a country that defends freedom as the core of American values, director Barbara Kopple explores the absolute powers of the FDA over access to investigational drugs that may be the only chance at survival for terminally ill patients." In this documentary, she further argued, "Patient and public safety is jeopardized when breakthroughs are lost or delayed by an insurmountable process—with a cost tallied in human lives. Through an intimate journey with patients, physicians, researchers, advocates and FDA overseers, Kopple asks the poignant question: "'What rights should you have in a life or death battle to survive versus what decisions should the government make for you? It's a question we all must answer before we each face our own Fight to Live.'" *Given my family's current medical situation, these motivating words, bolstered and inspired me.*

After viewing the film, Jimmy and I had the pleasure to personally meet with Ms. Kopple and discuss our purpose for attending the RDLA conference. The filmmaker was deeply moved by my account of Jason and Justin's *fight to live*. We had our photo taken with her, she gave me her business card, and suggested we keep in touch, *which I intend to do*. Jimmy and I left DC with a sense of newly acquired knowledge, a feeling of accomplishment, and anticipated hope. *What an informative and enlightening experience!*

CHAPTER FORTY-NINE

Knowledge is love and light
And vision.
~Helen Keller

AFTER *ELBOW RUBBING* with political and social activists, I was eager to return home to my wife and three children. I was anxious to share my incredible experience and new—found knowledge with Deena. Many thoughts and ideas where swirling around in my head. This new surge of energy made me realize even more that we had to continue to push in making a *major* difference for the MPS community. As we approached home, the onset of torrential rains failed to unnerve me. *The rain represented nourishment for my newly planted enthusiasm.*

When I arrived home, I was anxious to surprise Justin by picking him up at school confident that he would be just as excited to see me—*and he was*! When my son spotted me, his eyes grew bright and a huge smile beamed across his quirky, adorable face. The love and light beaming from Justin and later Jason's faces always gives me the courage to persevere. Immediately after our warm greeting, Justin and I rushed home to surprise Jason as he got off his school bus. He, too, was thrilled to see me. The three of us hugged, kissed, teased, and chattered up a storm. *It was a great reunion*! Similar to most families with children, my excitement was short-lived as the boys started to fight, complain, and, yes, *drive me crazy. I love my little tough guys!* The ever-present reality of their vulnerability and the insurmountable challenges we, as a family, must face every single day haunts me. Yet, as *Martin Luther King promised: "We Shall Overcome!"*

CHAPTER FIFTY

*Never doubt that a small group of thoughtful,
Committed citizens can change the world:
Indeed it's the only thing that ever has.*
~Margaret Mead

OUR LIVES DID not turn out the way we thought it would. But whose does? There is no idyllic life. Even though there are so many questions and uncertainties about the future which we face day after day, this *continuing journey* will not be in vain. What counts is that we take pride in the accomplishments we have achieved so far. Our voices were *heard loud and clear* at the RDLA conference. President Obama recently passed a bill for the funding of rare disease research. Currently I am working with NJ State Senator Nellie Pou, D-Hawthorne, on a bill that would require all newborns to be tested for Hunter syndrome/MPS II. If passed, it will be known as the "Let Them Be Little Bill." *No words will be adequate to describe our feelings if that bill passes and becomes law!* Changing a life, fighting for a worthy cause, gives us a sense of achievement and great pride knowing that our efforts will someday, *hopefully*, help to alleviate the pain and suffering affiliated with rare genetic disease.

Fear will not deter us. The late President Franklin Delano Roosevelt succinctly professed: "The only thing we have to fear is fear itself." Taking something positive from a negative and striving to make a difference is what keep us strong. This empowers and sustains us. Understanding and love have helped us cast aside the terror Hunter syndrome/MPS II brings to our lives. *Jason and Justin's story will carry on with the gift of each new day.*

It is important that Deena and I keep a watchful eye on our sons to be keenly aware of symptoms or complications as the disease progresses. It is imperative that we seek treatment to provide relief as their physical and mental health deteriorates. As a family, we continue to strive to let our boys be little—to run, sing, dance, and play. A new chapter can easily unfold at any given moment but here's where our story ends.

My wife and I knew the moment that we embarked on this unfamiliar path that we were going to experience heaven and hell, joy and pain, dreams and hopelessness. *With all our pain and suffering, Deena and I will always be joyful and thankful.* Deena and I end this portion of our journey with humble humility, immense gratitude, and endless love.

Jason, Justin, and Jordan are the light in our lives! Their *spectacular brilliance* guides us along this dark, treacherous road leading us toward renewed hope and discovery. *As travelers on this uncharted-transitional* journey, *we have changed and have been transformed—hopefully into better human beings who can make a difference in the world.*

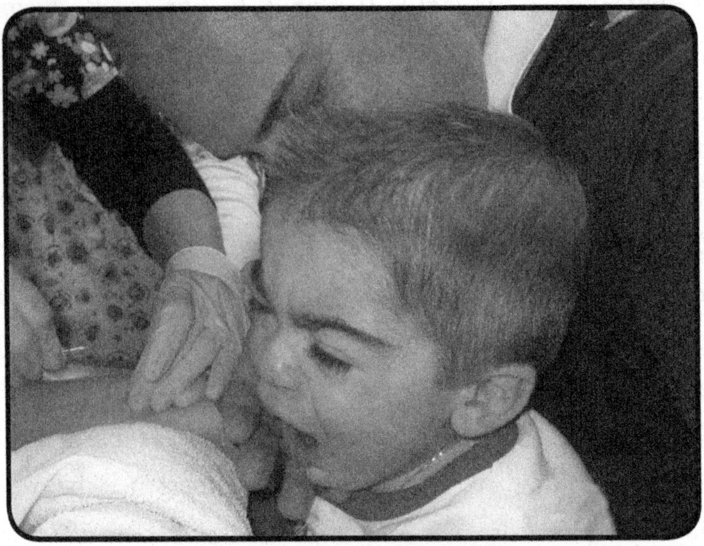

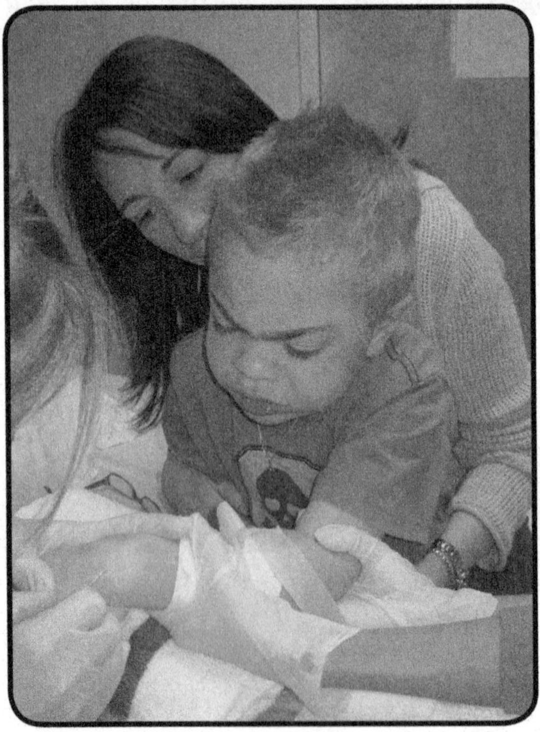

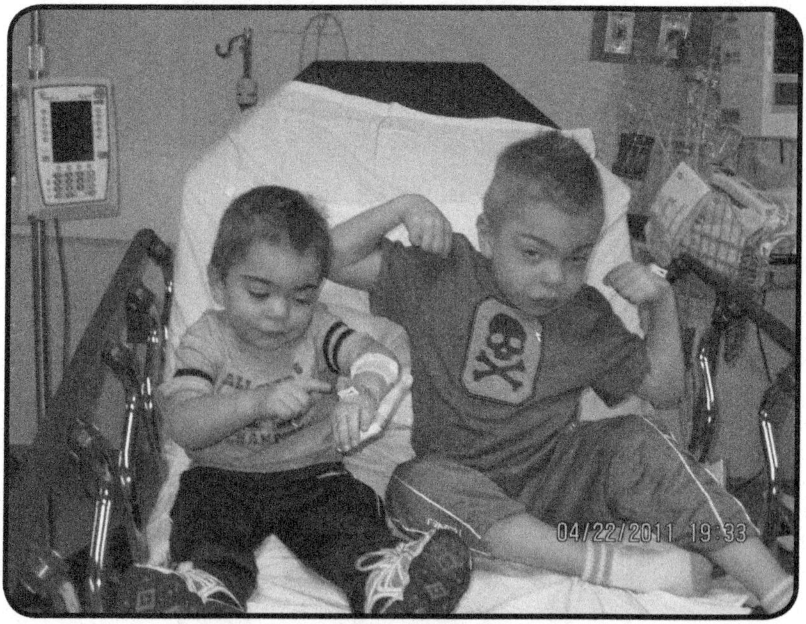
04/22/2011 19:33

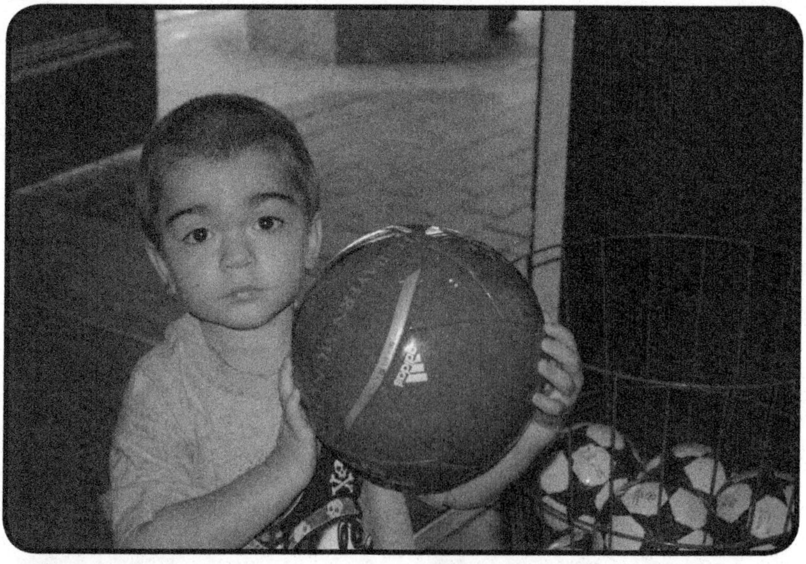

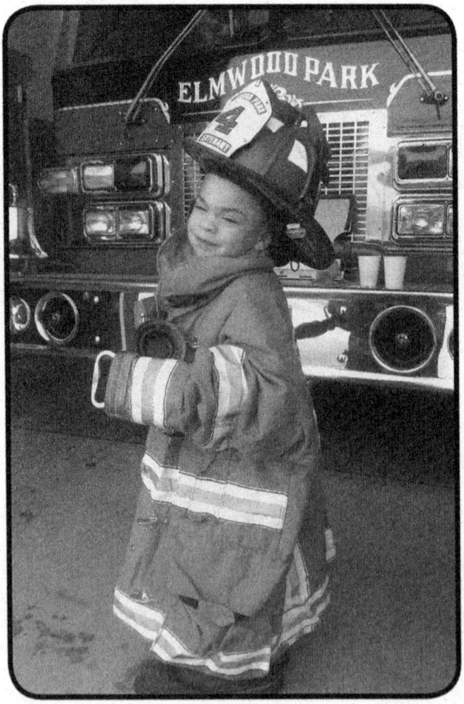
ELMWOOD PARK

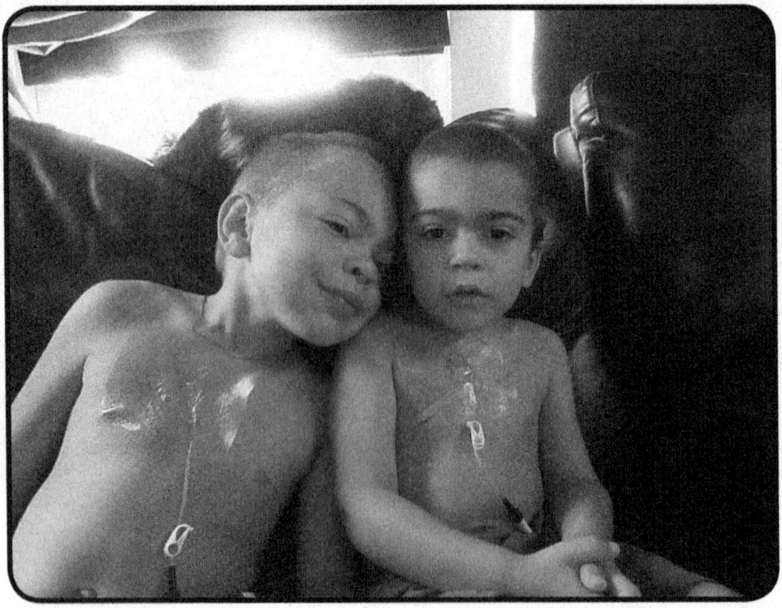

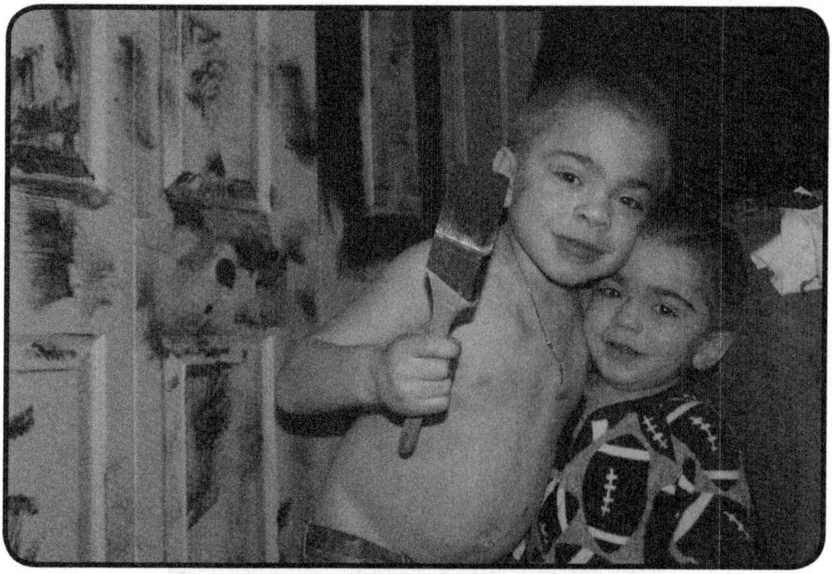

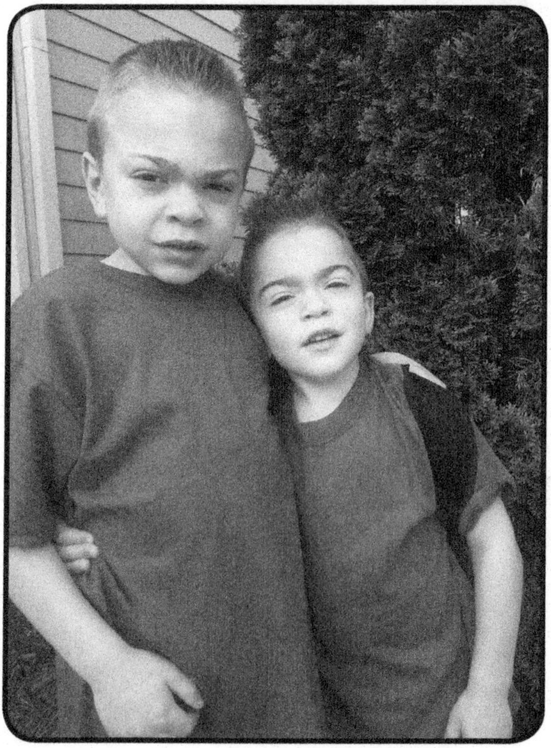

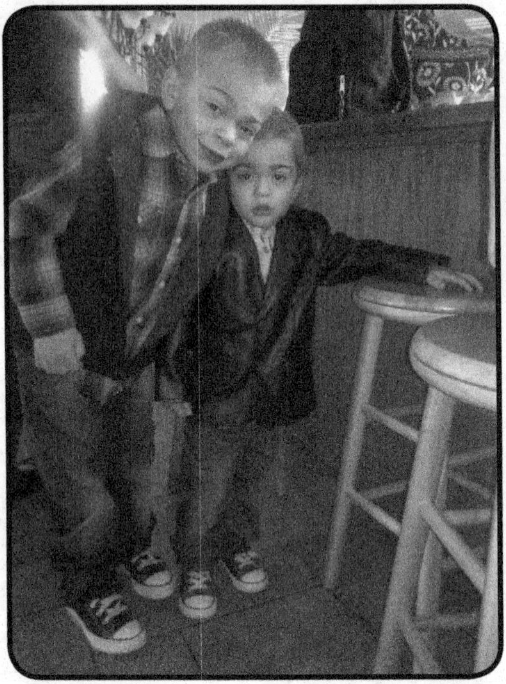

EPILOGUE

It's safe to say that nothing lasts forever.
This night cannot escape tomorrow.
We'll keep moving on.
Move through the storm until we see what we've become
When there's no road for us to follow,
We'll keep moving on. We'll keep moving on.
~Journey

THE LATE FRED Rogers, TV's lovable *Mr. Rogers*, beautifully professed: "Anyone who does anything to help a child in his life is a hero to me." Holding tightly onto Jason and Justin's hands, we continue on this course, not alone, but with exceptional friends and loyal supporters. Collectively and/or individually, they have blessed our lives with their rich love and selfless efforts. Some claim that we are "heroes" however, we believe that our two precious sons, our beautiful daughter, our loving family, our dearest friends (*on this earth or in heaven*), Geralyn Mancini (Jason and Justin's adored friend) and all the incredible people we have met along the way, they are *the special ones*. The brave children suffering with MPS and their devoted and courageous families—*are the true heroes!*

As I previously mentioned, our story will not have a happy conclusion but there is a positive aspect to telling this tale. Our book is the vehicle that will transport us on the road to finding a cure for Hunter syndrome/MPS II. Our hope for a brighter future for all those inflicted and suffering with rare genetic diseases will fuel our perseverance. *We'll keep moving on even if our shoes wear out. We'll keep driving forward and never run out of hope!*

Jason, Justin, and Jordan, Mommy and Daddy love you and always will!

Our Journey Continues . . .

*Happiness is not something ready made,
It comes from your own actions.*
~Dalai Lama XIV

Deena and Jeffrey Leider welcome you to follow them on their website: www.jasonandjustinsjourneyx2.com

Acknowledgements

Thank you to the following people for their inspiration, help, and support:

To a dear friend, Mary Ann Tesoroni, for generously volunteering her time editing this book so brilliantly and Jennifer Lota for her expertise on formatting the manuscript and her competent computer skills.

Especially, to the *courageous* Deena and Jeffrey Leider for opening their hearts and for allowing us the privilege to write their motivational and unique story.

A very special thank you to Jason, Justin, and Jordan, who made us laugh, cry and added much warmth to our lives. May they always "Be Little" and their days filled with laughter

About the Authors

Helena C. Farrell is a produced playwright, a member of the Dramatist Guild of America, and the Italian American Writer's Association. She is the writer of the original produced Off-Broadway, romantic comedy, "Room for Rent." She completed her doctorate studies in Literature with a concentration in Writing. Her latest book, "The Longest Goodbye: A Memoir," was published in 2009. She is currently working on her new novel, "No Trick or Treats," coming out soon. She lives in Glen Rock, NJ with her husband, Joseph T. Farrell, MD.

Geralyn A. Mancini received her Bachelor of Arts degree in Communication Studies from Fairleigh Dickenson University. She is the co-creator and Executive Producer of "Giselle the Global Girl," a local children's program that aired on TV34 Montclair, NJ. Currently she is working on creating Giselle into a children's book series and collaborating with Deena Leider on a children's book about heaven. She also donates her time to volunteer work for local and international children's charities. Geralyn resides in her hometown of Hawthorne, NJ.

CPSIA information can be obtained
at www.ICGtesting.com
Printed in the USA
BVOW03s0135140917
494867BV00001B/1/P

9 781491 819432